Great reviews for
Pamela Acheson and Dick Myers and
their *Best Romantic Escapes in Florida*
series

"If you don't happen to own a great romantic
escape, *The Best Romantic Escapes in Florida* is
the next best thing." —*Donald Trump*

"A near guarantee of a great trip."
—*Independent Publisher*

"A valid and nifty guide to wonderful places...and
a bunch of little things to make the trip especially
romantic." —*Naples Daily News*

Dick Myers and Pamela Acheson are two
"extraordinary writers." —*Fodor's Florida*

"*The Best Romantic Escapes in Florida* includes
tips for romantic surprises, a list of inexpensive
romantic extravagances and ideas for romance."
—*Orlando Sentinel*

"The focus is on romance, with tried and tested
hints and off-the-beaten-path destinations."
—*The New Smyrna Beach Observer*

"Pick up this book. It has a lot of great ideas."
— *News Center 6, Orlando*

Other Books by Pamela Acheson and Richard B. Myers

The Best Romantic Escapes in Florida, Volume Two

Other Books by Pamela Acheson

The Best of the British Virgin Islands
The Best of St. Thomas and St. John, U.S. Virgin Islands

Other Books by Richard B. Myers

Visiting the Virgin Islands with the Kids
Tennis for Humans: A Simple Blueprint for Winning
The Best of the Peter Island Morning Sun

THE
BEST ROMANTIC
ESCAPES
IN
FLORIDA
VOLUME ONE

**A Lovers' Guide to Exceptionally Romantic Inns,
Resorts, Restaurants, Activities, and Experiences**

THIRD EDITION

PAMELA ACHESON
RICHARD B. MYERS

TWO THOUSAND THREE ASSOCIATES

TTTA

Published by
TWO THOUSAND THREE ASSOCIATES
4180 Saxon Drive, New Smyrna Beach, Florida 32169
Voice: 1.800.598.5256 or 386.427.7876   Fax: 386.423.7523

Printed in the United States of America

Library of Congress Cataloging-in-Publication Data
Acheson, Pamela.
    The best romantic escapes in Florida : a lovers' guide to exceptionally
romantic inns, resorts, restaurants, activities, and experiences / Pamela
Acheson, Richard B. Myers.--3rd ed.
      p. cm.
    Includes index.
    ISBN 1-892285-06-1 (alk. paper)
    1. Florida--Guidebooks. 2. Couples--Travel--Florida--Guidebooks.
    3.Resorts--Florida--Guidebooks. 4. Hotels--Florida--Guidebooks.
    I. Myers, Richard B. (Richard Brooks), 1946- II. Title.
    F309.3 .A54 1999b
    917.5904'63--dc21   99-057979
                                                         CIP

Back Cover Photograph: Courtesy of VISIT FLORIDA

ISBN 1-892285-06-1

First Printing January 2003

For lovers everywhere

*A word from the editor about the authors' research
and the timeliness and accuracy of this book:*

The authors have stayed at every lodging choice in this book at least several times. They have eaten in every restaurant in this book many times. They have been to every shop, attraction, bistro, and balloon ride, etc. They have done all this anonymously.

They pay their own way.

The authors have also been to hundreds of hotels, inns, restaurants, nightclubs, and attractions that they chose not to put in this book.

Believe me, the authors have done their homework. And because they have devoted all their efforts to picking the very best and leaving out the rest, they have done your homework for you.

No establishment mentioned in this book has paid to be mentioned. No establishment has written or approved its own description.

Unlike many travel guides, this book finishes its final fact-checking process only three to four weeks before the book is on the shelves in your local bookstore.

The authors' books are the most current books in the industry when they hit the shelves and they are updated regularly.

—H.H.

ACKNOWLEDGEMENTS
Special thanks to Jon and Paige at Imagecraft and to Juli Maltagliati.

DISCLAIMER
The authors have made every effort to ensure accuracy in this book. Neither the authors nor the publisher is responsible for anyone's traveling or vacation experiences.

INTRODUCTION

This fully-revised and updated third edition of *The Best Romantic Escapes in Florida, Volume One* is for everyone who wants a romantic escape. It's for people who don't have any time and want to steal a quick weekend away. It's for people who want to spend a blissfully romantic ten days together. It's for people planning for a very special anniversary or simply celebrating a new day of being in love. It's for people who want some more romance in their lives.

The escapes in this book and the romantic suggestions are here to make your life easier. Romantic lodging choices are paired with romantic things you can do once you arrive. With this book, you and your partner can pick a destination and make a few phone calls and quickly be on your romantic way.

By the way, Florida is an incredibly romantic state. If you thought all the sunshine state had to offer were flashy theme parks, palm trees, and spring breakers, then you are in for a wonderful surprise.

The truth is, the two of us moved to Florida reluctantly, but we fell in love with it fast. In fact, we were dazzled. Great romantic restaurants and lodging choices abound. And it's one long romantic show for the senses here—vibrant sunrises, glorious sunsets, fragrant night-blooming flowers, salty ocean breezes, warm sun, giant moons that pop out of the sea, the lulling sound of lapping waves, the possibility of 70 degrees and sunny any day all winter long.

When could be a better time to go than now? So go find your partner and make time for a romantic escape—silk sheets and a shower together, sunsets on the beach, champagne or chocolate or flowers, floating together in the Gulf, a candlelight dinner for two, a dance in a crowd or a walk under the stars—whatever your romantic ideas, you'll find them here.

—P.A. and R.B.M.

TABLE OF CONTENTS

SPECIAL FEATURES

FLORIDA

MORE THAN 30,000 LAKES
8,426 MILES OF TIDAL COAST

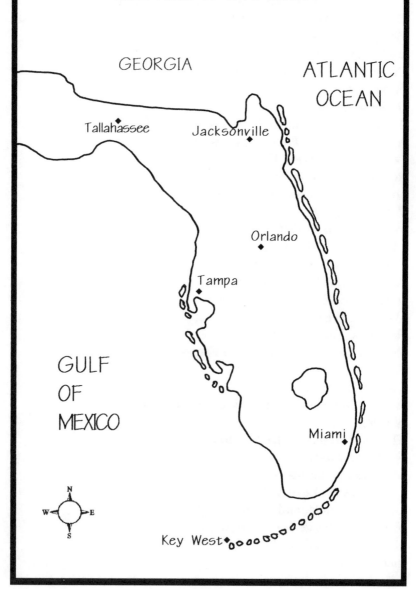

GEORGIA

ATLANTIC OCEAN

Tallahassee

Jacksonville

Orlando

Tampa

GULF OF MEXICO

Miami

N
W   E
S

Key West

CHAPTER 1

ROMANTIC FLORIDA

FLORIDA'S ROMANTIC SCENERY

Florida's scenery is made for romance. There are miles and miles of exquisite sandy beaches, quiet waterways, peaceful lakes, splashy rainbows, and a profusion of brilliantly colorful and fragrant flowers.

Photographs and paintings of Florida sunrises and sunsets look gaudy and unbelievable but in real life these morning and evening sky-shows are spectacular. A thousand shades of orange. A thousand more of pink. Crayola crayons wouldn't stand a chance.

Flat land makes for a big sky and at night Florida's sky turns into a giant, dazzling canopy of stars. It gets dark here at night (the way it doesn't in big cities) and the odd result is that it doesn't really get dark. On a moonless night the stars are so bright you can see easily along the beach. Constellations present themselves in astonishing detail. Planets look too big to be real. The more you look, the more you see. Speeding satellites, twinkling planes, sensational shooting stars.

In Florida, you are always near water. It's only two to three hours from the east to west coast and in the same day you could easily watch the sun rise out of the Atlantic and watch it set in the Gulf. When you stay on the east coast, you can catch the sun and the moon pop out of the sea. On the west coast, you can see both slip beneath the water.

Over 50 kinds of palm trees grow in Florida but other trees grow here as well. On Amelia Island giant old oaks draped with Spanish moss shade the streets. Many of the west coast beaches are lined with tall and graceful Australian Pines.

Inland is romantic, too. The most northern part of Florida is similar to Georgia—forests of tall pines, red clay earth, hills. Central Florida farmland is flat, with green pastures and fields that stretch for miles, rimmed in the distance by thick groves of trees.

If you don't know central Florida, the first time you look at a map you will think there has been a mistake—it looks as if a soda can exploded and splattered the map with mini-size drops. The truth is, those are all lakes. There are over thirty thousand of them in Florida. These lakes are very calm and peaceful to look at. Gentle mist rises off them in the early morning. At night they reflect the stars and the moon.

Summer is the time of spectacular afternoon and evening thunderstorms. On the west coast they roll right in. On the east coast off-shore breezes have daily battles with the storms that barrel across the state. Some days it rains all the way to the beach and other days it pours two or three miles inland but never makes it to the shore. These rains can be torrential, but last only minutes, and the strong sun dries up the traces.

FLORIDA'S GEOGRAPHY

Beaches run the length of the barrier islands that lie along most of Florida's east and west coasts. These islands protect the mainland from the Atlantic Ocean to the east and the Gulf of Mexico to the west. Between these islands and mainland Florida is the Intracoastal Waterway. Bridges, locally called causeways, connect most of these barrier islands to the mainland. Many of these are drawbridges, which open (at set times or on demand) for boats that are passing through.

Some of these islands are also connected to each other by bridges, but often you have to drive back to the mainland to get on to the next island. A1A is the name of the primary road that runs across all of these islands on the east coast. When you see a sign warning of the last exit to the mainland, that means, even if the road goes for 20 more miles, this is your last chance to get off the island.

In some spots the Intracoastal Waterway is quite narrow but in other places it winds through wide expanses of green and grassy marshes or acres of mangroves, and sometimes it is so broad that it is full of many little and mostly uninhabited islands. Two people can take peaceful canoe and kayak trips through these wetlands, and catch glimpses of rare birds, manatees, and dolphins.

FLORIDA'S WEATHER

In the summer, which runs from May through September, the weather is pretty much the same all over Florida—90s in the day, 80s at night. Breezes off the Gulf of Mexico and Atlantic Ocean keep the shores pleasantly cool and Florida's coasts are often considerably cooler in July and August than many northern cities.

Winter, however, is another matter. Temperatures in Florida can vary by an important ten degrees. The average high/low in February in Jacksonville is 66/46 and in Palm Beach it's 76/56. Many places in northern Florida have fireplaces that you can retreat to on chilly nights. During a rare cold snap temperatures at night can drop below freezing, even as far south as Palm Beach. On the other hand, on any given day, anywhere in Florida, all winter long, it can be high in the 70s and sunny.

FLORIDA'S ROADS

Florida's road system is made for traveling. An Interstate runs north-south along both sides of the peninsula and travel is easy along either coast. Several major Interstates cross the peninsula. Back roads are plentiful and more scenic. They can take much longer but can be fun.

FIND TIME TO GET AWAY TOGETHER

You only think that you don't have time for a romantic escape. No matter how busy and crazy your life may be, you actually do have the time.

And if you really don't, then it is time to make time. It is very, very important.

You don't have to make it a big deal. Start small, start at home.

Find time to be alone together. Hold hands and take a walk together after dinner, then take a bath or shower together after everyone else is asleep.

Get a sitter and go to a movie together and have an ice cream soda afterwards.

Plan an entire evening out regularly...it can be a trip to the mall and a snack at the food court or dinner at the nicest restaurant in town.

Plan a mini-escape. Just go have dinner or spend the night in the next town. It doesn't have to be a place in this book or even especially romantic on its own. It will feel like an incredible escape. All you need is a motel with a nice restaurant nearby. It could be a Holiday Inn near an Olive Garden. Try this some weeknight. You'll have a great romantic escape and not even miss work.

Make time and take time to make your life more adventurous, more romantic, and more fun!

©2003 by Pamela Acheson and Richard B. Myers from *The Best Romantic Escapes in Florida, Vol. One*

CHAPTER 2

ROMANTIC CHOICES

THE CHOICES

Florida is filled with wonderfully romantic escapes. There's something for everyone here. However, one person's romantic dream can be another person's nightmare. Also, romantic moods change. One time the two of you might be looking for an elegant retreat where you can be pampered and dine at lots of fine restaurants. Another time you might want to hide out in a private suite at a small inn, or retreat to an out-of-the-way Bed & Breakfast where you can spend your days walking on the beach.

There are all kinds of romantic escapes in this book. Some are sophisticated and refined. Others are laid-back. Some focus on an incredibly romantic lodging. In other destinations, it's really the entire experience that makes it romantic.

It's almost impossible to feel romantic if you are stressed, so everything in this book is designed to be easy. Although several destinations are fairly remote, they are reachable easily on a major highway and close to an airport. Virtually all of the places in this book were chosen partly because once you get there, you can stay there. There's either enough to do on the property or many things you can walk to, if you feel like doing something. Romantic restaurants are within walking distance of the lodging or just a short drive so you don't have to get lost or mixed-up about directions.

HOW THIS BOOK IS ORGANIZED AND HOW TO USE IT

The book divides Florida into three sections: the East Coast, Inland Florida, and the West Coast. Destinations within the sections are in geographical order, not alphabetical order. This enables you to compare places that are near each other.

Each chapter starts with an overview of the destination. This is followed by a description of the most romantic lodging choice in the area, romantic places to dine, and suggestions of things to do.

Don't be startled if all the places in this book seem romantic. They are. That's the whole point of the book. The non-romantic places have been weeded out for you. You don't have to try to read between the lines to figure out if a certain place is actually romantic. All of these destinations are special and wonderful and romantic.

However, each destination is romantic in a different way. It's classier, or calmer, or cozier, or more remote. Sometimes it's the lodging itself that is incredibly romantic. Other times it is the experience of the whole destination. So choose what the two of you want.

Start by reading the overviews. Circle the words that appeal to you. Write "no" on the ones you don't like. Then look in more detail at the destinations that entice you. Then give the book to your partner and have your partner do the same thing (using a different color ink). Or go through the book together.

Or if you are already heading to a Florida destination (to visit parents or children, or for business reasons), this is the perfect time to attach that trip to a romantic escape. So look up destinations close to where you are headed . . . and sneak away together or meet there.

16

SECTION 1

FLORIDA'S ROMANTIC EAST COAST

AMELIA ISLAND
JACKSONVILLE
PONTE VEDRA BEACH
ST. AUGUSTINE
DAYTONA BEACH
NEW SMYRNA BEACH
COCOA BEACH
PALM BEACH
DELRAY BEACH
FORT LAUDERDALE

◆ROMANTIC EAST COAST DESTINATIONS

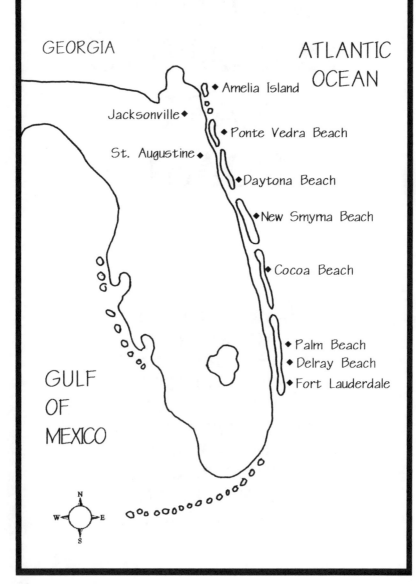

GEORGIA

ATLANTIC OCEAN

◆ Amelia Island

Jacksonville ◆

◆ Ponte Vedra Beach

St. Augustine ◆

◆ Daytona Beach

◆ New Smyrna Beach

◆ Cocoa Beach

◆ Palm Beach
◆ Delray Beach
◆ Fort Lauderdale

GULF OF MEXICO

CHAPTER 3

A ROMANTIC ESCAPE TO AMELIA ISLAND

AN OVERVIEW

This slender island is a remote and peaceful hideaway even though it's less than an hour north of Jacksonville. Majestic sand dunes, some as high as 30 feet, rim a stunning 13-mile-long beach.

The tiny town of Fernandina Beach is on the west side of the island on the Intracoastal Waterway. Here you'll find restaurants and shops and a remarkable 50-block area of Victorian houses built in the late 1800s when this was a prosperous shipping community. Streets are lined with towering old oaks draped with Spanish moss.

There are two exceptionally romantic properties here. If the two of you want to be right on the beach in a luxury resort that you never have to leave, choose the Ritz-Carlton Amelia Island. If you prefer to stay in an elegant Bed & Breakfast and walk to restaurants and shops and don't mind if the beach is over a mile away, head for the restored, and incredibly romantic, Fairbanks House in Fernandina Beach.

LODGING FOR LOVERS
RITZ-CARLTON AMELIA ISLAND

Come to this very elegant, self-contained, oceanfront resort for superb cuisine, gentle pampering, a spacious room, and nightly entertainment plus miles and miles of almost empty, windswept beach.

The beautiful drive here through grassy tidal marshes is a romantic prelude to the relaxation to come. Hold hands and take in the scenery. Once you arrive, you never have to leave, although the wide beach beckons for long morning walks and nighttime stargazing.

Rooms are hallmark Ritz-Carlton with classy, comfortable furniture and plenty of space. The two of you can stay in bed for days, ordering from room service and listening to the lulling sound of the ocean (which you can see from your bed). Or check in to the private-access Club Floor and relax in the living room and enjoy five complimentary food presentations daily (when one ends, another begins) and endless beverage service (including liquor, wines, and champagne).

Dine elegantly in The Grill, the resort's peerless restaurant (open Tuesday through Saturday), or the very casual Cafe 4750, which is open for all meals, and even has take-out. Do order breakfast in your room or out on your terrace where you can enjoy the stunning view.

For the darkest and most intimate bar, step into the one at The Grill and listen to the soft music of the piano. The very large and very elegant Lobby Lounge has several rooms and many seating arrangements and it's easy to find a private place for the two of you to sit. Head here after dinner for a spin around the dance floor, or find a dim and quiet corner and just listen to the nightly entertainment. There are miles of beach to explore and a state-of-the-art spa with a spacious indoor pool.

2 restaurants, 2 bars, 24-hour room service, billiards, golf course, tennis courts, indoor and outdoor pools, spa. Dress code: No tank tops, torn jeans in public areas, no shorts in the evening. Jackets required in The Grill. Non-smoking rooms available. Check-out noon. 449 rooms. 4750 Amelia Island Pkwy., Amelia Island, 32034. Res: 800.241.3333. Tel: 904.277.1100. Fax: 904.261.9063. Web: www.ritzcarlton.com $169-$339 $15/day valet parking

20

THE FAIRBANKS HOUSE

At this sophisticated Bed & Breakfast the rooms and suites are romantic retreats, many with their own electric fireplaces. It's not on the beach, but there is a lovely pool. Town and some of the best restaurants on the island are short walks away.

This restored 19th-century Italianate villa, which is individually listed in the National Register of Historic Places, is set way back from a quiet street, amidst exquisitely manicured lawns, brilliant flower beds, and tall old oaks draped with Spanish moss.

There are nine rooms and suites in the main house and three cottages. All units are romantic and are decorated with mixes of patterned wallpapers, deep hues of paint, oriental rugs, and antiques. If you want to spend a lot of time in your room, the first and second floor suites are the best choices. Both are quite spacious, with a comfortable living room, a separate bedroom with a walk-in closet, and a bath with both stall shower and jacuzzi. The first floor suite has a private entrance. All units have coffee makers and many also have little fridges for your beverages and snacks.

The white terry robes and turndown service with a chocolate treat are nice touches. Some rooms have electric fireplaces and some have jacuzzis and some have both. If the two of you want a full gourmet breakfast (served from 8-9:30 a.m), choose a place at the dining room table or a private table on the romantic little porch and service will begin. After breakfast you can stroll hand in hand through the gardens or relax in the comfortable living room with the newspapers or sit by the pool. The peaceful center of town is just a few blocks away and you can walk or bike to restaurants, shops, and boat rides. You can also bike to the beach. At cocktail hour, guests gather for complimentary beverages and hors d'oeuvres. For a truly romantic treat, arrange for a carriage ride to dinner and be sure to inquire about the special two- to seven-night romantic packages.

Pool, bikes. No smoking on property. No children under 12. Check-out 11 a.m. 9 rooms and suites, 3 cottages. Innkeepers: Bill and Theresa Hamilton. 227 S. Seventh St., Amelia Island, 32034. Res: 800.261.4838. Tel: 904.277.0500. Fax: 904.277.3103. Web: www.fairbankshouse.com $160-$285

21

RESTAURANTS FOR LOVERS
BEECH STREET GRILL
Tables are in a number of rooms on both levels of this charming and romantic two-story house built in 1889. Although romantically dark, this spot can be somewhat noisy when crowded, so for an intimate dinner ask for a quiet table. A pianist plays upstairs Thursday through Saturday. The cuisine is a creative mixture of southern, Asian, and hip. Crab cakes and sesame-seared ginger tuna make fine appetizers. Local shrimp stuffed with crab, grilled duck with ancho chili, and Portuguese fish stew over linguini are excellent entree choices. The wine list is great. *Dinner nightly. 801 Beech St., 904.277.3662 $$-$$$*

JOE'S 2ND STREET BISTRO
Romantics in the know make this a must-stop destination. Choose a table on the upstairs balcony or an umbrella table on the walled-in brick terrace or dine inside where it's dark and tropical plants and deep green walls hung with art provide a peaceful background for an evening of romance. You might start with the broiled shrimp, or the crab cakes, or Joe's spicy gumbo. Fresh local seafood is a specialty here but the breast of duck, rosemary lamb chops, and grilled filet are a taste treat. End the evening with champagne sabayon and a glass of port. *Dinner Tues.-Sun. 14 S. 2nd St., 904.321.2558 $$-$$$*

LE CLOS
Step into this charming little yellow and white cottage for a truly delightful romantic dinner. Candles grace the tables in this dimly lit, intimate room that is painted deep red with white trim. The framed menu hangs on the back wall and nightly specials are inscribed on a blackboard. Cuisine here is pure Provencale. Come for the escargot, the pate, the coquelles St. Jacques, the tender seared duck, and the braised lamb shank. French wine lovers will find the inspired list a true pleasure. *Dinner Mon.-Sat. 20 S. 2nd St., 904.261.8100 $$-$$$*

ROMANTIC THINGS TO DO HERE
Explore the 50 blocks of astonishingly ornate Victorian houses. They were built by wealthy sea captains and merchants who tried to outdo each other in conspicuous opulence.

Share a slab of chocolate peanut butter, chocolate walnut, or rocky road fudge at Fantastic Fudge *(218 Centre St., 904.277.4801).*

Hop into Old Towne Carriage Company's *(904.277.1555)* horse-drawn carriages for a romantic ride for two in town or out to the beach.

Go on a sunset cruise for two. Sail Amelia *(Fernandina Marina at west end of Centre St.,904.261.9125)* offers two-hour sailing cruises.

Take a biplane ride over Amelia Island or over Cumberland Island with Island Aerial Tours *(1600 Airport Rd., 904.321.0904).*

Ride horses on the beach. Call Sea Horse Stables *(904.261.4878).*

Stop by O'Kane's Irish Pub *(318 Centre St., 904.261.1000)* to hear talented local groups who really know how to sing and play instruments.

Dine at Who's on Fourth *(22 S. 4th St., 904.261.7700)* weekends and listen to the owner play a sweet guitar.

Watch the sun at Brett's Waterway Cafe *(Marina, 904.261.2660).*

Find sparkling glass fusion pieces and other original delights at Sax North 3rd Street *(11 N. 3rd St., 904.277.4104).*

Boat over to Cumberland Island for dinner at the Grayfield Inn *(904.261.6408)* or for a day of deserted beaches and a picnic provided by the inn. Advance notice is required.

Take a canoe ride together. You'll find canoe and hiking trails at Big Talbot Island State Park just south of Amelia Island on A1A.

ROMANTIC RADIO
Light rock: 96.1FM   Jazz: 97.9FM

HELPFUL HINTS: If you stay at the Ritz-Carlton, bear in mind that valet parking is mandatory and guys need jackets to dine in The Grill.

Directions: I-95, exit 373. East on A1A (Sr 200)13 mi. to Fernandina Beach.

A FEW OF THE MANY REASONS FOR LOVING FLORIDA

A BURGER ON THE BEACH

SAND IN YOUR SHOES

PELICANS DIVE-BOMBING FOR LUNCH

SHRIMP

MORE SHRIMP

FROZEN DRINKS

THE GIANT SKY

MANATEES AND DOLPHINS

FABULOUS BEACHES

SPECTACULAR CLOUDS
AND LIGHTNING SHOWS

MANGROVES AND MARSHES

CHAPTER 4

A ROMANTIC ESCAPE TO JACKSONVILLE

AN OVERVIEW

The St. Johns River cuts a broad path right through the center of Jacksonville, a sprawling city with many distinct neighborhoods. High-rise buildings are clustered in the compact downtown area, but just ten minutes to the south is the splendidly peaceful residential section called Riverside. If it weren't for the cars offering a clue to the decade, you could easily think you had dropped back to an earlier era.

For serenity and solitude at a very romantic Bed & Breakfast, head to the beautifully-restored Plantation–Manor Inn in Riverside. This is the place to come when the two of you feel like hiding away and just resting. There's nothing much to do here except relax in your room, or perhaps sit on the porch, or go down to the beautiful pool, or make occasional forays out for a meal.

You can take a walk but there's really nowhere to walk to. The tiny (one block long) and charming village of Avondale, with several good restaurants and one-of-a-kind shopping, is just a five-minute drive away, and a great piano cafe is nearby.

LODGING FOR LOVERS
PLANTATION-MANOR INN

Built in 1905, this stately mansion is an exceptionally classy, quiet retreat. There's almost nothing to do. The two of you can talk, sleep, read, wander down to the pool, take a short drive to a restaurant for lunch or dinner. Rooms are beautifully decorated, well insulated from noise, and designed to be stayed in.

As you turn into the driveway, you feel as if you've driven into an incredibly peaceful sanctuary. Ahead are well-spaced parking nooks, each for a single car. To the left is a stately mansion, surrounded by trees, with massive Greek Revival Doric columns supporting a second-floor wrap-around veranda.

The entire building, including magnificent cypress woodwork, has been painstakingly restored and thick insulation between rooms insures privacy. Indeed, even with televisions on, each room is a sanctuary. The nine rooms are lavishly decorated—mixes of wallpapers, fancy draperies, canopy beds, armoires, frilly linens.

All the rooms here are romantic in one way or another but they are very different from each other. One has a giant bathroom with a window seat for two, an old-fashioned tub that the two of you can soak in (cozily), and a modern shower. Another has a separate sitting area. Since each room is so different, it's best to call to see what is available and then decide what you want. There's one room on the first floor. Five rooms are on the second floor and three are on the third floor.

On the first floor are several elegantly decorated (but very comfortable) living rooms and a dining room where a full breakfast is served at a large table. The mansion is set back from the road and there are lawns to walk on outside. A tall fence insures privacy at a long and pretty lap pool surrounded by a brick patio and shaded by leafy trees.

Pool, whirlpool. No smoking inside. No children under 12. Check-out 11 a.m. 9 rooms. Owners/Innkeepers: Kathy and Jerry Ray. 1630 Copeland St., Jacksonville, 32204. Tel: 904.384.4630. Fax: 904.387.0960. Web: www.plantationmanorinn.com $150-$180

A RESTAURANT FOR LOVERS
STERLING'S OF AVONDALE

Paintings adorn the deep-hued walls at this sophisticated restaurant where a flickering candle on each cloth-covered table hints at the romantic evening to come. The two of you can dine inside looking out to the avenue, but the most romantic seats are in the intimate room in back or the outdoor courtyard beyond. The menu is eclectic—try the fried green tomatoes, or escargot, or crisp calamari for appetizers; move on to the chef's specialty: filet Victor, a pan-seared filet with a cabernet reduction, wild mushrooms, and sweet onions. It's quiet here even when it's crowded and this is an excellent choice for a romantic lunch or dinner. *Lunch, dinner daily. 3551 St. Johns Ave., 904.387.0700 $$-$$$*

FOR AN EVENING OF PIANO
STELLA'S PIANO CAFE

Belly up to the baby grand for a cocktail before dinner, or stop by after for dessert and a cordial. The music starts at 5:30 p.m. and goes until 10 p.m. during the week and 11 p.m. on Fridays and Saturdays. *1521 Margaret St., 904.353.2900*

A ROMANTIC STROLL

For a look at what towns used to be like years ago, head three miles south to the tiny center of Avondale. It's just one tree-lined block long and amazingly quiet. There are only original shops and restaurants, none of the chains that have taken over so many main streets. Spend an hour just slowly browsing. **White's of Avondale** (*3563 St. John's Ave., 904.387.9288*) is a terrific independent bookstore where you can find great greeting cards, stationery, and gifts, as well as books. Indulge yourselves at the **Peter Brooke Chocolatier** (*3554 St. John's Ave., 904.387.3827*) and stroll the avenue with an ice cream cone.

ROMANTIC RADIO
Soft rock: 96.1FM   Jazz: 97.9FM

HELPFUL HINTS: This is a great place to stay in your room and relax.

Directions: Going north on I-95, exit at Riverside Ave (US 17). Go over river, turn left on Riverside Ave. (15 blocks) to Copeland St. Turn right on Copeland.

27

Practical Packing for Lovers

Body paint – for the artist in all of us

Massage oils with sunscreen

A small flashlight

A scented candle or two – to enhance dinner or bath

Something special and sexy for your partner to wear

Insect repellent and some Sting-Eze (just in case)

Lip "stuff" with SPF – this is no time for chapped lips

Tapes, discs, videos if appropriate

Midnight snacks, some juice, other beverages

A couple of hats or bandannas

A surprise for your lover – that you both can enjoy

*A little stash of cash or travelers checks
for a special splurge*

CHAPTER 5

A ROMANTIC ESCAPE TO PONTE VEDRA BEACH

AN OVERVIEW

Ponte Vedra Beach, which is right on the coast 20 miles southeast of Jacksonville, has been developed residentially as an upscale winter community and there are acres and acres of attractive and pricey houses but no real town of any sort.

Tucked amidst this development and right on the beach is the delightfully romantic Lodge & Club at Ponte Vedra Beach. This is the place to come when the two of you want to stay in one place and just chill out and do nothing but you also want to be able to walk right out to the beach, and you want the amenities that only a complete full-service resort can provide.

Here you two can settle into a room with a fireplace and a jacuzzi, step outside to the beach, cross the street to a full-service spa, wander into the comfortable lounge and listen to quiet music, and dine in the oceanfront restaurant. When you feel like finding shops or more restaurants, they're just a five-minute drive away.

LODGING FOR LOVERS
THE LODGE & CLUB AT PONTE VEDRA BEACH

The spacious suites overlooking the ocean with jacuzzis and gas fireplaces plus the beachfront location are the romantic draw here.

With only 66 rooms, this full-service resort manages to have an intimate feel, although club members who live in the area can and do use the facilities. Rooms are in a tight cluster of four-story Mediterranean-style buildings with orange tile roofs. You'll find that the Ocean Suites are comfortable, romantic havens. Although actually one big room, the cathedral ceiling, cozy window seat, angled four-poster king bed, and kitchen area (with microwave, small fridge, and coffee maker) create a feeling of several rooms.

A gas fireplace open on two sides lets you enjoy the fire from the bed as well as from the sofa. These are accommodations made for romance. Slip out of your clothes and into the thick cotton robes you'll find in the closet. The spacious marble bathroom features a shower big enough for two as well as a separate two-person tub or jacuzzi.

Everything is easy for lovers here. There's 24-hour room service, the elegant Innlet Restaurant overlooking the ocean, and a seasonal poolside restaurant. The Innlet Lounge, which also offers meal service, features a pianist on Thursday, Friday, and Saturday evenings. High Tea and Sherry are offered each afternoon. Thanksgiving and Christmas buffets here are outstanding—elegant and uncrowded.

There's close to a mile of sandy beach and three pools, including one just for adults. There's a service charge of $10 a day and 18% is added to your meal and beverage charges but additional tipping is not allowed. Not only do you come out about even, it's very relaxing to just sign your name.

Restaurant, bar, 24-hour room service, 3 pools, spa, kayaks, bikes. Non-smoking units available. Check-out noon. 66 rooms and suites (32 with gas fireplaces). 607 Ponte Vedra Blvd., Ponte Vedra Beach, 32082. Res: 800.243.4304. Tel: 904.273.9500. Fax: 904.273.0210. Web: www.pvresorts.com $200-$450

A RESTAURANT FOR LOVERS
TRA VINI RISTORANTE
It's an easy drive to this elegant and intimate Italian restaurant and its excellently-prepared cuisine and extensive menu. Tables are on two levels and there is a comfortable bar. Begin with the calamari stuffed with spinach, or polenta with roasted peppers and provolone, or share a shitake mushroom pizza. For entrees, it's a tough choice. Veal marsala, or a superbly grilled veal chop, or perhaps the shrimp and capellini. You can't go wrong. *Dinner nightly. 216 Ponte Vedra Park Dr., 904.273.2442 $$-$$$*

ROMANTIC THINGS TO DO HERE
Go horseback riding along the beach. Talk to anyone at the front desk and they will make arrangements with a nearby stable.

Have a bonfire on the beach, a specialty here. It may sound odd but they're wonderfully romantic. For a price you can have your own private bonfire along with after-dinner cordials and even a violinist.

Don't miss the chance to experience the award-winning cuisine at Restaurant Medure (*818 N. A1A, 904.543.3797*), owned and operated by the famed Medure brothers.

Sail for a half- or full-day on a luxurious 65-foot motor yacht from Comanche Cove, which is about 15 minutes south at Vilano Beach.

Watch a movie and order up munchies—pizzas, popcorn, cheese board—from the roomservice movie munchie menu.

ROMANTIC RADIO
Easy: 96.1FM   Jazz: 97.9FM   Oldies: 102.9FM

HELPFUL HINTS: Many northerners come to their Ponte Vedra Beach houses for the winter and, during this time, restaurants are busy, usually dressier, and you will definitely need a reservation.

Directions: I-95, exit 344. East on 202 (Butler) to A1A. Go south 3 mi. to left on Corona. Turn right at Ponte Vedra Blvd. and drive south to Lodge.

WHAT IS ROMANTIC?

While researching this book literally thousands of couples from age 16 to 92 were asked: "What is the first thing that comes to mind when you hear the word 'romantic'?" The most common responses were: candlelight dinners, the full moon, flowers, chocolate, diamonds, and champagne. But there were many other, more "individualized" responses, all listed below. Why not add a few of your own?

flying kites	hugs
sitting by a fire	naps
Sinatra	martinis
sharing pajamas	wrestling
mirrors	limos
weekends	midnight
ribs	crying
waterbeds	sharing wine
pizza	hammocks
skinny-dipping	big bathtubs
showering together	whipped cream
brunch	violins
poetry	tan lines
thunderstorms	sandy feet
the past	matinees
phone booths	no tan lines
oysters	sweat
room service	elbows
doing nothing	Kenny G
sex	smiling
fun	Elvis
vacations	holding hands

CHAPTER 6

A ROMANTIC ESCAPE TO ST. AUGUSTINE

AN OVERVIEW

St. Augustine is located in northeast Florida, set on the mainland and facing the Intracoastal Waterway. Founded in 1565, it is the oldest continuously occupied European settlement in the continental United States. The compact downtown area of St. Augustine contains a remarkable collection of historical buildings, some dating from as early as the 1500s (Ponce de Leon discovered this area in 1513).

This is a place for lovers to explore. There's one of the country's best preserved forts, the oldest wooden schoolhouse in the country, a number of fascinating museums, and a two-square-block, re-created Spanish village complete with "interpreters" re-enacting 18th-century life. St. Augustine is an extremely popular destination, and on weekends especially, streets and walkways can be crowded with visitors. Luckily, set right in the heart of the historic district is the splendidly romantic Casa Monica Hotel. Built in 1888, and once owned by Florida magnate Henry Flagler, this castle-like escape is a perfect retreat for lovers.

LODGING FOR LOVERS
CASA MONICA HOTEL

Set in the heart of an historic city, this "castle," built well over a century ago, is a thoroughly modernized and appealing romantic retreat from the hustle and bustle outside.

The Casa Monica Hotel opened in 1888 and from then until the early 1930s it thrived as a fabulous winter retreat for wealthy northerners. Traveling south with trunks full of fancy gowns and dinner jackets, guests spent the chillier months living at the hotel and dining and dancing at charity balls and elegant parties. The Depression put an end to the frivolity and the hotel remained closed until the mid-1960s when it reopened as the county courthouse. Then, in 1997, work began to transform the building back into the luxury escape that it is today.

The hotel is a grand structure covering nearly half a city block. The exterior has been fully restored to its original design. In the style of a Moorish Revival castle, it includes kneeling balconies, hand-painted Italian tile, arched windows, and five towers, the tallest reaching up seven stories. Luxurious two-story suites are tucked into the towers and they showcase stunning views of the city.

The entrance is through an elegant lobby with marble floors, Moorish archways and columns, chandeliers from Syria, tropical ferns, and a fountain. Suites and rooms have been completely modernized and are decorated with Spanish-style furnishings: Picard-pattern draperies, wrought iron beds, wicker lounge chairs, mahogany tables. All rooms have coffee makers and safes.

On the second story, a large pool is set in a courtyard. For a romantic evening, dine at the hotel's 95 Cordova Restaurant and stop by the dimly-lit Cobalt Lounge before or after. For $15 each, beach lovers have guest privileges at the Serenata Beach Club, ten minutes away.

Restaurant, bar, deli, room service 6 a.m.-10 p.m., pool, exercise room, gift shop. Non-smoking rooms available. Check out 11 a.m. 138 units. 95 Cordova St. at King St., St. Augustine, 32136. Res: 800.648.1888. Tel: 904.827.1888. Fax: 904.819.6065. Web: www.casamonica.com $149-$269

RESTAURANTS FOR LOVERS
95 CORDOVA

For a truly romantic evening slip into this enchanting Moroccan-decorated spot in the Casa Monica Hotel. The eclectic menu includes a delightful mix of culinary creations: Asian, Cajun, French, contemporary, and just plain southern. For appetizers, try the Asian crab and shrimp stack, or the wild mushroom risotto, or a cup of smoked chicken gumbo with Italian white beans. Then move on to the crispy cashew salmon, or the seafood strudel with sesame asparagus, or the unusual but superb olive-and-blue-cheese-crusted N.Y. strip. For dessert, double chocolate cake, apple pie, or creme brulee are sweet choices. *Breakfast, lunch, dinner daily; Sun. brunch. 95 Cordova St., 904.810.6810 $$-$$$*

ROMANTIC THINGS TO DO HERE

Check out the Castillo de San Marcos *(1 E. Castillo Dr., 904.829.6506)*, which took over 25 years to build. It is a beautifully preserved 300-year-old fort, complete with drawbridge and dungeons.

Catch some blues and jazz at the Flamingo Room at Cortesse's Bistro *(172 San Marco Blvd. across from Library Park, 904.825.6775)*. There's entertainment Wednesday through Sunday, starting at 7:30 p.m, at this bistro and espresso bar.

Create your own art gallery tour for the two of you. Look for the brochure "Art Galleries of St. Augustine" which includes a map and description of 20 art galleries you can walk to in the downtown area.

Step way back in time and watch cobblers, blacksmiths, carpenters, and candle makers go about 18th-century daily life in the two-square-block Spanish Quarter Village *(29 St. George St., 904.825.6830)*.

ROMANTIC RADIO
Jazz: 97.9FM Easy: 96.1FM Classical: 88.5FM Country: 105.5FM

HELPFUL HINTS: Beware that this is a tourist town, and you will generally encounter crowds on the streets day and night even in the off-season.

Directions: I-95, exit 311. Go on 207 to US 1. Turn left. Turn right on King St.

DO NOT DISTURB
AND A FEW OTHER "DO'S"

Do bring a "do not disturb" sign with you in case there's not one in the room. Of course you can call down for it, but you usually want it because you don't want to be disturbed.

Do bring your music with you. Sony makes a great little radio-CD player that's about five inches square and an inch thick. It's got great sound and even runs on batteries.

Do protect Florida's beaches. Don't walk on or play in the sand dunes or pick sea oats. It's a Florida law. What you wreck in a few minutes may never, ever come back.

Do unplug that little clock radio as soon as you check in so the two of you won't get wakened at 4 a.m. to the previous guest's choice of music.

Do marvel at how lucky it is that with over two billion people on this planet, you two managed to find each other.

Do go outside at night. As this side of the earth spins away from the sun, a sparkling nightscape appears. Look for shooting stars and satellites.

Do go down to the beach together just before dawn at least once. You probably won't see any other people and the light changes are stunning.

Do look at rainstorms in the distance. Sometimes you can be driving directly toward the storm—you can see the sheet of rain just ahead. And then the road turns and you aren't in it after all but you can see the rain just 20 feet away.

©2003 by Pamela Acheson and Richard B. Myers from *The Best Romantic Escapes in Florida, Vol. One*

CHAPTER 7

A ROMANTIC ESCAPE TO DAYTONA BEACH

AN OVERVIEW

Daytona Beach is on the northeast coast of Florida. It is certainly a town more known for the Daytona 500, Bike Week, and Spring Break than for romance. And indeed, during motorcycle and automobile events, the town might be called exciting or even thrilling, but certainly not traditionally "romantic." However, away from all the special events, crowds, and cacophony, there is also a relaxed, romantic side to the "world's most famous beach" that remains undiscovered by most.

Several blocks of downtown Beach Street have been streetscaped with wide brick sidewalks and there are a couple of restaurants and bars and some shops. By the way, Beach Street, despite its name, is not on the beach but instead, actually runs along the mainland side of the Intracoastal Waterway.

Just a half-mile further south on Beach Street, facing the Intracoastal Waterway and set under a canopy of live oak trees, is the charmingly restored Live Oak Inn and its own romantic restaurant, Rosario's.

LODGING FOR LOVERS
LIVE OAK INN

This historic 10-room inn is a charming spot for a romantic escape. It's across from the city marina and looks out to boats and the Intracoastal Waterway. There's an excellent restaurant right downstairs.

The inn is actually in two restored frame houses that sit side-by-side surrounded by shade trees in a quiet residential neighborhood across from the city marina. Both buildings are listed in the National Register of Historic Places. One was built in 1871 and is the oldest existing building in Volusia County. The other, built in 1881, is the oldest existing house in Daytona Beach. The site of the inn is said to be the site where Mathias Day founded Daytona.

These are truly old houses and stairs creak and floors squeak. Rooms vary in size but many are large and decorated with a mix of period antiques and more contemporary furnishings. Some of the rooms have jacuzzis and some have separate sitting areas and little private outdoor porches—a fine spot for a nightcap under the stars. Windows look out across the marina to the Intracoastal Waterway or to manicured gardens and trees.

If the two of you want to spend a lot of time inside your room, you might want to opt for the spacious Bill France Room with a claw tub in the bathroom and a jacuzzi in an alcove at the other end of the room. The very quiet and sizeable Day Room also has a jacuzzi.

In the morning come down and enjoy breakfast at a table for two in the sunny white breakfast room or out on the porch. There are several common living areas and complimentary wine and tea is served in the afternoon. The inn is set in a quiet residential area, good for walking. Although there is no pool, the beach is just a five-minute drive away. All this helps make the Live Oak Inn a wonderful place to truly get away from it all.

Bikes. Smoking outside only. No children under 13. Check out noon. 10 rooms. Innkeeper: Lynn Smithers Hubbard. 444-448 S. Beach St., Daytona Beach, 32114. Res: 800.881.4667. Tel: 386.252.4667. Fax: 386.239.0068 $80-$160

A RESTAURANT FOR LOVERS
ROSARIO'S

When the two of you feel like a romantic evening, head to this Italian restaurant, which occupies the first floor of the Live Oak Inn. Tables are charmingly arranged in several rooms. Italian-born chef/owner Rosario performs nightly magic in the kitchen while his wife Sunny deftly manages the dining room. You might begin by sharing the antipasto. Fine entrees include the spaghetti putanesca with sun-dried tomatoes, olives, capers, and anchovies; veal marsala; or scampi alla Rosario. Specials include his popular, whiskey-infused Beef Manhattan. *Dinner Tues.-Sat. 448 S. Beach St., 386.258.6066 $$-$$$*

ROMANTIC THINGS TO DO HERE

Look at all the gracious coquina stone homes along Palmetto Street. Just walk one block west.

Have a drink looking out at the Intracoastal Waterway at the Chart House bar *(645 S. Beach St., 386.255.9022)*, a pleasant walk away.

Take a cruise together. A Tiny Cruise Line *(401 S. Beach St., 386.226.2343)* offers a delightful excursion that leaves just across the street. When they say tiny, they mean tiny. This smooth, quiet 1890's style launch carries a maximum of 14 but they "always run, even with one," so you two might even have the boat to yourselves. Daytime cruises run year-round; the sunset cruise from April to October.

Take a backstage tour through the Angell and Phelps Candy Store and Chocolate Factory *(154 S. Beach St., 386.252.6531)*. The aroma is intensely chocolate (even the air must have calories here!).

Check out the architecture of the old Post Office on Beach Street.

ROMANTIC RADIO:
Jazz: 97.9FM   Easy: 1230AM   Classical: 88.5FM   Rock: 93.1FM

HELPFUL HINTS: If you seek peace and quiet on this escape, be sure there are no special events in town, unless, of course, the event is part of your plan.

Directions: I-95, exit 261. East on US 92 to Beach St. Turn right (south).

CEREMONY & CELEBRATION

A wedding isn't just a wedding. It is a wedding ceremony. An anniversary isn't just an anniversary. It is an anniversary celebration. These are a couple of "big ones" but it only takes some minor adjustments to turn ordinary events into romantic ceremonies and celebrations. Try these at home or on your next romantic escape.

Light a candle, get out the good glasses, and turn a take-out pizza eaten on the couch into a romantic meal.

Pause and make a toast to your lover before you start a meal; it's a romantic ceremony you can even do at breakfast.

Pack a picnic and bring napkins and silverware instead of stopping at a fast food restaurant on a trip. Find a quiet park and share a picnic together.

Getting dressed together for an evening out can be both a ceremony and a celebration. Put on some music, share a glass of wine or an early dance, and then button her blouse, help him into his jacket, tie his tie.

Choose a special wine or a dessert to share and turn a meal together into a special celebration.

Celebrate all kinds of smaller anniversaries together: the day you found your first apartment; the night you knew you were in love; the day you decided to get married.

Dance together when you hear a song that means something to both of you. Do this whether you are in the kitchen or the shower or even walking down the street.

When you wake up in the morning, hug each other and ask the question "How are we going to celebrate our love and the joy of being alive (and together) today?"

CHAPTER 8

A ROMANTIC ESCAPE TO NEW SMYRNA BEACH

AN OVERVIEW

Northeast of Orlando, on the northeast coast of Florida, is little New Smyrna Beach. It's split down the middle by the Intracoastal Waterway and the beachside half of town is unusually isolated and protected. In fact, it's the only town in the state of Florida to share a barrier island with a National Seashore and to have an unbridged inlet to both the north and south. Only the two bridges that cross the Intracoastal from mainland New Smyrna provide access to this unpretentious beach town. This is a unique situation that hopefully will be preserved.

It's the whole experience of being in New Smyrna Beach more than any one thing that makes a trip here romantic. There's a 20-mile-long beach, more than half of which is in the Canaveral National Seashore; the Atlantic Center for the Arts and its art gallery; plus many casual restaurants and surf shops. The hard sand beach is wide and great for walking, although you must watch out for the cars that are allowed on parts of the beach during the day. At night the beach is almost always empty and a romantic place to watch for shooting stars. The charmingly restored Riverview Hotel is definitely the romantic place to stay.

LODGING FOR LOVERS
RIVERVIEW HOTEL

You can spend time in your comfortable room or out by the pool at this appealing and romantic inn. When you feel like taking a walk, the brick sidewalks of Flagler Avenue are right out the door, leading to restaurants, art galleries, shops, and the beach.

A brick walkway leads to this charming three-story inn, which is set back from the Intracoastal Waterway and just a stroll from the Atlantic Ocean. The inn is surrounded by bright flowers and tropical shrubbery, and giant old oak trees create welcome shade. A wide veranda wraps around two sides of the building, and comfortable rocking chairs almost call out to have you come and set a spell.

A drawbridge crosses the Intracoastal Waterway here and the inn was originally built in 1885 as the bridge tender's home. There's still a drawbridge, although it's been modernized several times, and the home was thoroughly restored in 1984 and turned into a delightful inn.

The building has a Florida-style tin roof and is painted bright pink with white balconies and gingerbread trim. Comfortably decorated rooms vary in size and all but one have a porch or balcony. Furniture is a mix of wicker and oak. The two third-floor honeymoon suites have four-poster beds and one has a nice view of the waterway. Breakfast is served in your room or on your balcony.

The common living room has been turned into an art gallery and just past the registration desk is a wonderfully imaginative gift shop. A bougainvillea-covered fence hides a large and lovely private pool. Next door, overlooking the water, is Kelsey's Riverview Restaurant and Bar. In the other direction is Flagler Avenue's eclectic mix of shops and galleries. Along with its great location and inviting decor, Riverview Hotel's caring innkeepers are romantics at heart.

Restaurant, bar, pool, bikes, gift shop. Check-out noon. 19 rooms. Innkeepers: Jim and Christa Kelsey. 103 Flagler Ave., New Smyrna Beach, 32169. Res: 800.945.7416. Tel: 386.428.5858. Fax: 386.423.8927. Web: www.riverviewhotel.com $95-$200

A RESTAURANT FOR LOVERS
SPANISH RIVER GRILL

Hidden in the corner of a shopping center is this intimate and romantic jewel of a restaurant, the best in New Smyrna. It's owned and run by award-winning chef Henry Salgado and his charming wife Michele. Some of the cuisine is classic Cuban and Spanish, but other selections are highly original fusions, drawing on Florida-southern, Asian, and French ingredients and techniques. Come here to dine on outstandingly fresh fish, to sample such Cuban specialties as black bean soup and chorizo-stuffed rib eye, or to feast on a fabulous filet. Be sure to check out the creative specials, which can run the gamut from Asian-style soft-shell crabs to seared tuna over a freshly-made salsa to pork tenderloin with garlic mashed potatoes. Save room for Michele's remarkable flan and end the meal with a glass of aged port. *Dinner Tues.-Sun., lunch seasonally. 737 E. Third Ave., 386.424.6991 $$*

ROMANTIC THINGS TO DO HERE

See the current showing at Arts on Douglas *(123 Douglas St., 386.428.1133),* a stylish art gallery just across the bridge on the mainland. If you're in town the first Saturday of any month, stop in between 4 p.m and 7 p.m. for the classy reception (it's free).

Walk to ultra-casual Toni and Joe's *(309 Buenos Aires, 386.427.6850)* for lunch on the beach. Come in a bathing suit and bare feet. It's just south of the lifeguard tower. T&J's may look basic but the beers are ice-cold and the cheesesteaks the best anywhere.

Dine on the wonderful deck at Kelsey's Riverview Restaurant *(101 Flagler Ave., 386.428.1865)* and listen to Gino Conti sing love songs.

Pick up a plate of icy cold, cooked shrimp with cocktail sauce from Ocean's Seafood *(601 E. Third Ave., 386.423.5511)* to take to the beach or back to your porch. Do sample the homemade dips.

Walk or bike along the beach for miles and miles. The swimming is easy (but be careful when the surf is up). Please don't play or walk in the fragile dune system or pick any sea oats. It's very harmful to the environment (and it's also against the law).

Get your hair cut together at Sandy Beach *(404 Flagler Ave., 386.427.6211)*. Ask for Sandy. She's great!

Stop by Beach Buns *(300 Flagler Ave., 386.428.7700)* for scrumptious baked goods, pastries, or tasty sandwiches. You can sit inside or out.

Drive down to the Canaveral National Seashore's beautiful beach. For details on trips and activities, call the Park Ranger *(386.428.3384)*.

Share a delicious pastry or tasty pie or fabulous sandwich from delightful Mon Delice *(730 Third Ave., 386.427.6555; 307 Flagler Ave., 386.427.0153)*, Serge and Pam's authentic French bakeries.

Pick up a bouquet for your room or have flowers sent as a surprise the day you get home. Just call or stop by the Pink Flamingo at Petals *(810 Third Ave., 386.423.5927)*.

Check out the enticing array of hand-crafted items at Global Crafts *(300B Flagler Ave., 386.424.1662)*, which helps artisans in developing countries sell wares on the internet (www.globalcrafts.org). Sample the daily brew of free-trade coffee and then buy some to take home.

Look for a great gift at Ocean Village Treasures *(306 Flagler Ave., 386.428.3008)*. Stop by their Christmas annex.

Dine under the stars at Chase's on the Beach *(3401 S. Atlantic, 386.423.8787)*. See the fiery glow of night shuttle launches here.

Browse through Palms Up Pottery *(413 Flagler Ave., 386.428.3726)* for a colorful and creative selection of cups, bowls, and platters.

ROMANTIC RADIO
Easy: 107.7FM   '40s to '80s: 1230AM Oldies: 105.9FM

HELPFUL HINTS: This is a casual town, day and night, and it closes up early during the week. To preview the surf "live" log onto www.oceanviewcam.com.

Directions: I-95, exit 249. East on SR 44. Cross Intracoastal Waterway and left onto Peninsula Dr. Left onto Flagler Ave.

"DON'T BE SILLY!"

You have finally escaped together for some intimate and romantic experiences. You are away from the weight and stress of everyday life. This is obviously no time to be silly. You are adults. You should not do anything even remotely resembling the following. Certainly you wouldn't do them together. Don't be silly and . . .

walk in the rain

sing songs in the car

laugh out loud until you both cry

talk incessantly about why you love each other

stay up all night talking and hugging

go out for an ice cream cone, two scoops each

neck on the plane

kiss in the elevator

hold hands for your entire trip

fall asleep together under a tree

order eggs Benedict

have a Bloody Mary

take silly or risque photographs

send even sillier postcards to friends and family

lie together outside silently and just listen to life

eat a donut in the middle of the day

have a pillow fight

create a love poem for your lover

dance until your feet hurt

DECLARATIONS
OF LOVE

Create an "official" gift certificate to be redeemed for a massage from you, or a shampoo, or a car wash — whatever your love would like.

Have a T-shirt or a hat or a bumper sticker made (check the Yellow Pages under silk screening/screen printing) that lets everyone and each other know you're in love: "Greatest Lover," "Love of My Life," "We may be old but we're still madly in love," etc.

Get a trophy made for your love. Award it for "Making My Life Wonderful" or "Best Spouse in the History of the World." It can be serious or silly.

Make a sign for the desk or the car or the boat shed that declares your love.

Hire a skywriter to draw your message of love across the afternoon sky.

Hire one of those aerial banner beach planes to fly up and down the beach saying "I love Suzy" or Fred or whoever your love is.

Write "I love you" on yellow post-it notes and secretly stick them all over the house—inside the medicine cabinet, in drawers, in closets, in the refrigerator—so your love will find them all day long.

Write "I love you" in shaving cream on the mirror.

CHAPTER 9

A ROMANTIC ESCAPE TO COCOA BEACH

AN OVERVIEW

Cocoa Beach is on one of the Atlantic's barrier islands about an hour south of New Smyrna Beach, an hour north of Vero Beach, and an hour east of Orlando. This is a busy beach town that is better known for surfing and the amazing world famous Ron Jon Surf Shop than for romance.

But just a block east of the bustle of A1A, in a remarkably quiet oceanfront setting, is The Inn at Cocoa Beach. This family-owned, mid-sized, four-story inn may look large, but it feels like an intimate Bed & Breakfast. The guest rooms are spacious, there is a cozy library with a fireplace, a peaceful fountain, delightful gardens, and a beautiful private pool. All this, plus the beach just a few steps away, makes this a one of a kind romantic escape.

From the serenity of the inn, you can stroll the beach or check out the numerous lively beach bars, see the sunset over the Intracoastal Waterway, and then enjoy fine dining accompanied by live romantic piano music.

LODGING FOR LOVERS
THE INN AT COCOA BEACH

Charming and very romantic, this oceanfront inn is a delightfully peaceful oasis for lovers.

A quiet street leads to the manicured grounds of this four-story inn that faces the Atlantic. The Deluxe rooms are definitely the romantic choice here. They are unusually large, with ample room for the sofa and chair seating arrangement plus another table and two chairs, and are individually decorated with reproduction antique furniture, including four-poster beds. Some have two-person jacuzzis and some have fireplaces. All have private balconies that showcase the ocean. The two of you can sit here at night and watch the moon pop out of the ocean or catch a space shuttle launch.

The inn offers many relaxing venues. Settle into a sunchair on the large deck around the pool or find a shady seat on the brick patio and listen to the gurgling fountain as you gaze out at a beautifully manicured lawn hedged with sea grapes. There are several living rooms and a library with a fireplace. The second-floor sundeck is a peaceful place to catch some daytime rays or nighttime star shows. To reach the beach, just walk through the gate near the pool.

In the morning, head down to the spacious breakfast room, where you can dine at a table for two inside or on the quiet porch. Guests are given a tray graciously arranged with glasses of juice, a plate of freshly baked breads and muffins, and fruit. Coffee, tea, other breads, and boiled eggs are also available. At the end of the day, join other guests at cocktail hour for wine and cheese.

Coffee and tea are always available and a handy honor bar offers sodas, bottled water, various beers, a wide array of liquor and liqueurs, plus a selection of champagnes and wines by the bottle.

Pool, fitness room, bikes, shuffleboard, massage (fee). Non-smoking rooms available. Check-out 11 a.m. 50 units. Owner: Karen Simpler. 4300 Ocean Beach Blvd., Cocoa Beach, 32931. Res: 800.343.5307. Tel: 321.799.3460. Fax: 321.784.8632. Web: www.theinnatcocoabeach.com $135-$295

A RESTAURANT FOR LOVERS
MANGO TREE

Oriental rugs grace the floors and framed oil paintings and dramatic stained glass sconces decorate the walls of this classy and romantic restaurant. Lovers have a choice of four delightful rooms in which to dine, including an enchanting glassed-in patio that looks out to lush tropical greenery and to a pond with swans swimming about. A pianist plays throughout the evening. The traditional menu includes rack of lamb, shrimp scampi, filet mignon with bearnaise sauce, and yellow fin tuna. *Dinner Tues.-Sun. 118 N. A1A, 321.799.0513 $$-$$$*

ROMANTIC THINGS TO DO HERE

Spend the day or evening in Cocoa Village *(Rt. 520 to the mainland; left on Brevard Ave.).* Browse the art galleries and appealing shops, stop for an ice cream cone, walk to the park. For an elegant, romantic lunch, dinner, or Sunday brunch don't miss the **Black Tulip** *(207 Brevard Ave., 321.631.1133).* **Bello Mondo** *(405 Delannoy Ave., 321.633.7653)* features fine Italian cuisine. For jazz, head to **Big Daddy Dave's Jazz and Blues Club** *(105 Harrison St., 321.638.1370).*

Cruise through the remarkable Ron Jon Surf Shop *(4151 N. A1A, 321.799.8888)* even if you don't surf. It's amazing.

Rent a pontoon boat and explore the Intracoastal Waterway. Call Turtleback Watersports *(321.784.1670).*

Check out Coconuts *(2 Minutemen Cswy., 321.784.1422)* to be in a crowd, the **Sunset Waterfront Cafe** *(500 W. Cocoa Beach Cswy., 321.783.8485)* for a sunset drink on the deck, the **Heidelberg** *(7 N. Orlando Ave., 321.783.6806)* for jazz, and the **Italian Courtyard** *(350 W. Cocoa Beach Cswy., 321.783.0413)* for pizza .

ROMANTIC RADIO
Easy: 107.7FM   Jazz: 103.1FM   Oldies: 105.9FM!

HELPFUL HINTS: During shuttle launches, it can be tough to get a room.

Directions: I-95, exit 201. Go east on 520. Cross A1A and continue one block. Turn right on Ocean Beach Blvd. to the inn.

AN INN, A RESORT, A BED & BREAKFAST
WHICH IS RIGHT FOR YOUR ROMANTIC ESCAPE?

RESORTS

Full-service resorts often have hundreds of rooms and always offer a complete array of services. You'll generally find a concierge, several restaurants and lounges, a spa and fitness center, 24-hour room service, a pool and/or a beach, tennis courts or a golf course or both, internet connections, in-room movies, and more.

Basically everything you could possibly want is right there on the property. Because they are larger and "everything" is right there, full-service resorts are busier than an inn or B&B. They are elegant and wonderful, but can be a bit less intimate once you leave your room.

INNS

Inns generally have between 20 and 120 rooms and were originally built to be inns. With the exception of the Governor's Inn and the Inn at Cocoa Beach, all the inns in this book have a restaurant on the property.

Many have room service available and will happily arrange for services that they themselvesdo not provide.

Inns do not offer the range of services that one finds in larger resorts. Instead they offer a bit more charm and calm than their full-service sisters, a more intimate atmosphere when you leave your room.

BED & BREAKFASTS

Bed & Breakfasts range from as few as five rooms to about a dozen. Most were originally built and used as private homes. Although there are restaurants nearby and some B&Bs can arrange for dinner to be served in your room, the B&Bs in this book do not have restaurants on the property.

Obviously you get a comfortable bed and a delicious breakfast but you will also get much more. With a B&B, your experience will be more like staying at a friend's home.

The innkeepers at the B&Bs in this book are as special as the properties. They have a genuine interest in making your stay with them as romantic and as special as it can possibly be.

> **"There is nothing which has yet been contrived by man by which so much happiness is produced as by a good tavern or inn."**
> – *Samuel Johnson*

A FEW ROMANTIC EXTRAVAGANCES

Extravagance is sexy and romantic...and, of course, expensive. But you're in love so you might want to take part in one or more of the following extravagant temptations.

Travel by limo. Have a limousine pick you up at your hotel and take the two of you out for a night on the town. Check with the concierge or the innkeeper for a limosine service. It's a treat to be driven around.

Rent a fancy car. Get a Corvette or a Jaguar or a convertible. If you're going to be driving, you might as well enjoy it.

Crash on the Club Level. If you've chosen a resort with a "club level" floor, go for it. It is more expensive but well worth it if you love food, beverages, and convenience.

Charter your own plane. Whether you want to land closer to your destination at a small local airport or actually at your destination (if it is Chalet Suzanne), a chartered flight can be a beautiful and romantic way to travel.

Swing for the suite. Whether it's the Honeymoon Suite or just an upgrade, what better time than now?

Go for the bubbles. Enjoy champagne or caviar or oysters or whatever is very special and celebratory for you both.

Splurge on flowers. Really splurge. If your love loves roses, order a dozen for the porch, a dozen for the bedroom, a dozen for the living room. Don't forget a dozen for the bath, too.

Get front row tickets to a concert, play, or sporting event.

CHAPTER 10

A ROMANTIC ESCAPE TO PALM BEACH

AN OVERVIEW

Palm Beach, on Florida's southeast coast, is refined and flashy at the same time. Landscaping is gorgeous here and tall, perfectly-clipped hedges conceal palatial estates. On famous Worth Avenue, the quintessential draw for conspicuous consumers, luxury cars and limousines parade past pricey jewelry stores and designer boutiques.

Come to this romantic escape to experience the superb service, to enjoy the cuisine in the elegant restaurants, to have a cocktail or two in the sophisticated lounges, and to dance together cheek-to-cheek all night long. Yes, Palm Beach can be expensive, but if you come May through October, it can be quite affordable.

The two most romantic lodging choices in Palm Beach are the very refined and classically elegant Chesterfield Hotel, on a tree-lined street two-and-a-half blocks north of Worth Avenue, and the historic Colony Hotel, just off of Worth Avenue, a block from the beach, and home of the legendary Polo Lounge, where the rich and famous have been entertained for more than sixty years.

LODGING FOR LOVERS
THE CHESTERFIELD HOTEL

When you're in the mood for a superbly elegant romantic escape check into this jewel just off Worth Avenue. From the exquisite service and decor to the sexy, X-rated Leopard Lounge ceiling, it's one-of-a-kind.

The two of you will think you've somehow crossed the Atlantic when you check into The Chesterfield. Built in 1926, it underwent many transformations until 1989 when the owners of several classy London hotels purchased the property and imbued it with classic British style.

All units in this four-story hotel are stunningly and individually decorated (watch for the leopards, which turn up everywhere). Some rooms are small but the detail of the decor and the high ceilings turn them into cozy and romantic retreats. For a special splurge, the junior suites and full suites are outstanding. There's a spacious living area or separate room, plus a CD player and VCR. Some have two bathrooms. Or go for the lavishly decorated penthouse, on the fourth floor all by itself and reached by a private stairway. All units have fridges with complimentary bottled water and soft drinks.

Head to the large pool in the quiet courtyard or peruse the daily papers in the gracious wood-paneled library with a fireplace and comfortable leather furnishings. In the afternoon, enjoy High Tea—in the library, by the pool, or in your room. For any service, just ask the concierge.

Dine elegantly at breakfast, lunch, or dinner in the intimate Leopard Restaurant. Have a cocktail and share a dance together in the Leopard Lounge, where there is nightly entertainment. Take a good long look at the sexy, X-rated ceiling. Room service is always available and elegantly served (try lunch in bed for a special treat). There's no need to venture outside the Chesterfield, but if you do, sophisticated shops and restaurants are just a few blocks away.

Restaurant, bar, 24-hour room service, pool, library. Non-smoking rooms available. Check-out noon. 54 units. General Manager: Francine Boissonneault. 363 Cocoanut Row, Palm Beach, 33480. Res: 800.243.7871. Tel: 561.659.5800. Fax: 561.659.6707. Web: www.redcarnationhotels.com $99-$435

THE COLONY HOTEL

Newly-renovated rooms (some with ocean views), Worth Avenue shopping and dining just around the corner, and the beach a block away, make this historic hotel, which is home to the legendary Polo Lounge, an excellent romantic choice.

A Palm Beach landmark, the six-story Colony Hotel is painted pale yellow with white trim and flanked by tall and stately palms. Celebrities, from movie stars to politicians to the wealthy jet set, have made this their Palm Beach stop for more than sixty years.

All rooms and suites have been recently remodeled and redecorated. Some units on the higher floors have lovely views of the ocean while others overlook lush and tropical greenery. If you are on an extra-special romantic retreat, consider staying across the street in one of the seven luxurious two-bedroom townhouse villas with jetted tubs and full kitchens. That is, if you can get one. These are often rented out for the entire season, and sometimes guests have been known to stay a full year.

Start your evening with a cocktail or a glass of champagne at the popular Polo Lounge and Restaurant. One night, stay for dinner; the next night, dine elsewhere and come back to the Polo Lounge to dance. A group plays Thursday, Friday, and Saturday evenings. For breakfast or lunch, choose a window table or sit outside around the large swimming pool. One night have dinner and catch the show at the Colony's Royal Room Cabaret.

Saks Fifth Avenue and Neiman Marcus are just around the corner. Spend your days wandering the avenue, stopping to lunch along the way. Laze around either pool (hotel guests are welcome at the main pool and the very quiet pool behind the villas) or walk a block to the beach or rent bikes at the Bell Stand and follow the Lake Trail.

Restaurant, bar, cabaret, room service 6 a.m.-10 p.m., 2 pools, hair salon. Non-smoking rooms available. Check-out noon. 90 units. General Manager: Roger Eberingham. 155 Hammon Ave., Palm Beach, 33480. Res: 800.521.5525. Tel: 561.655.5430. Fax: 561.832.7318. Web: www.thecolonypalmbeach.com $130-$375

A RESTAURANT FOR LOVERS
RENATO'S

Service is impeccable at this small and enchanting spot that is a short walk from the Chesterfield and the Colony. Just inside the entrance is a tiny bar and a white piano, and a pianist plays softly as you dine in romantic elegance. Flowers are on each table, the atmosphere is hushed, and it is easy to forget that anyone else is around. So gaze into each other's eyes, share a bottle of excellent Italian wine, and enjoy classic Italian cuisine served on Limoges porcelain. For starters, the bresaola with goat cheese, the unusually light but excellent minestrone, or the roasted red peppers are good choices, but you really can't go wrong. Pastas and entrees are superbly prepared. You can also dine outside under the stars. It's a romantic place for lunch, too. *Dinner nightly, lunch Mon.-Sat. 87 Via Mizner, 561.655.9752 $$-$$$*

ROMANTIC THINGS TO DO HERE

Enjoy a light but elegant lunch or a fancy dinner at Trevini Ristorante *(upstairs at the Esplanade, 150 Worth Ave., 561.833.3883).* The menu is creative Italian, the ambience elegant, and the service outstanding, beginning with the gracious greeting as you arrive.

Come to the legendary Ta-Boo *(221 Worth Ave., 561.835.3500)* for brunch, lunch, or dinner, or even a late night dance. There's piano until 10 p.m. nightly, a DJ weekends from 11 p.m., and a great bar where the fish entertain you.

Relax in the shade at the peaceful Earl E.T. Smith Preservation Park *(S. County Rd. at Chilian Ave., just north of Worth Ave.)* where a wide circle of benches is nestled against a restful haven of tropical foliage.

Dine leisurely together at the romantic and ultra-chic Cafe L'Europe *(331 S. County Rd., 561.655.4020).* Choose an intimate banquette in the more formal mahogany-paneled dining room or a window table in the slightly more casual bistro room, or slip onto a bar stool for champagne and caviar. From the ahi tuna to the beef tenderloin, the quality and preparation of the offerings and the excellent service make this one of the best restaurants in the U.S. There's a jazz combo weekends. This is an elegant lunch stop, also.

Step back into the '50s and have an old-fashioned hamburger at Hamburger Heaven *(314 S. County Rd., 561.655.5277)*.

Dance under the stars at Chuck and Harold's *(207 Royal Poinciana Way, 561.659.1440)*. A portion of the roof actually folds back, opening up to the night sky. You lovebirds can dance under the stars!

If you've slept very late and want a quiet lunch in the afternoon, slip into a banquette at Bice *(313-1/2 Worth Ave., 561.835.1600)*. They serve all day and you are likely to have the place all to yourselves. This is a classy stop for lunch or dinner or a drink at the bar.

Dance Thursdays through Saturdays to the group at the Polo Lounge in the Colony Hotel *(155 Hammon Ave., 561.655.5430)*.

Fantasy window shop along Worth Avenue. Most of the things you can buy on this avenue are stunning, but so are the prices. So create a romantic fashion fantasy for two. First perhaps some buttery-soft leather shoes for each of you at Ferragamo. Head to Van Cleef & Arpels for your diamonds. Trillion carries gorgeous men's and women's cashmere sweaters in a rainbow of colors. You might as well opt for them all. Of course, you'll need a new suitcase for all this stuff, so you'd better make your last stop Louis Vuitton. To re-enter reality, share a bottle of bubbly at Ta-Boo, and toast to the money you saved.

Get all dressed up. It's sophisticated here and it's romantic to be dressy. So pack your sexiest heels and your wildest ties and have fun primping and "getting ready"—together—for a romantic evening.

ROMANTIC RADIO
Jazz: 93.9FM Classical: 92.1FM Soft Rock: 104.3FM Big Bands: 1420AM

HELPFUL HINTS: Palm Beach is one place in Florida where people really dress up. In season jackets are the norm for dinner. Off-season, you can get away with a more casual look, but why not have fun and wear your fancy clothes?

Directions: I-95, exit 70A. East on Okeechobee Blvd. over Royal Park Bridge. Turn right on S. County Rd. to Worth Ave. For the Colony, cross Worth Ave. to left entrance. For the Chesterfield, turn right on Worth Ave. to Cocoanut Row and go north three blocks.

COOL THINGS TO LOOK FOR

Millions of visitors come to Florida each year to see stuff yet they still miss some of the most amazing "stuff" you can see. Then again, maybe they aren't lucky enough to be in love and on a romantic escape.

THE GREEN FLASH. Catch it at sunset on the Gulf. You'll need a cloudless horizon to have a chance. Watch for a burst of emerald green just as the sun slips into the sea. There's no "maybe" about this one. When you see it, you really see it.

DOLPHINS PLAYING IN THE ATLANTIC. And the Gulf and all along the Intracoastal Waterway. These creatures are magnificent and you will notice that they are usually traveling with a "significant other."

SHOOTING STARS AND SATELLITES. Whether you're on a beach, or by a lake, or in a park, Florida seems made for stargazing. Search for the constellations, wait for a shooting star, track down a satellite, or just hold hands and wish upon a star.

SPECIAL SHELLS. Look for Florida's special "gifts."

GRASSHOPPERS TO GECKOS. Great grasshoppers, little lizards, and a bevy of bugs are on parade all the time.

SUNRISES AND SUNSETS. They're ridiculously gaudy.

PELICANS FLYING IN FORMATION OR DIVING FOR DINNER. And sandpipers standing on one leg and looking silly, or the solitary beauty of a heron feeding as evening descends along the shore.

CHAPTER 11

A ROMANTIC ESCAPE TO DELRAY BEACH

AN OVERVIEW

Almost everything—boutiques, art galleries, restaurants, jazz clubs, an historic hotel—in this compact and sophisticated little town is on a one-mile stretch of tree-lined Atlantic Avenue. It's never really crowded, although it can be busy. Delray Beach, which lies between Palm Beach and Fort Lauderdale on the southeast coast, is much quieter, for example, than Fort Lauderdale.

Delray's romantic stop is the historic Colony Hotel & Cabana Club. It was built in 1926 and, until 1997, open for only three months a year, during the winter. The hotel was a favorite tropical escape for wealthy northerners who wouldn't dream of staying less than the entire season. In the spring the staff traveled north to Kennebunkport, Maine to run the sister hotel for the summer (also called the Colony). Now only some of the staff travel back and forth and the Colony Hotel & Cabana Club in Delray Beach is open year-round. Come here if the two of you like the idea of staying in a quaint, rambling, old-fashioned, family-run hotel and want to walk easily to art galleries, restaurants, outdoor cafes, and the beach.

LODGING FOR LOVERS
THE COLONY HOTEL & CABANA CLUB

This romantic landmark has been run by the same family since 1930 and you can feel the history when you walk in the door. Walk back out, and all that Atlantic Avenue has to offer awaits you.

You feel the romance and the history the moment you enter this three-story, white stucco, Mediterranean-style hotel. The large lobby is filled with comfortable groupings of couches and you can imagine northerners gathered here years ago to while away the afternoon playing canasta. On the walls are photos of the owner's parents and grandparents and snapshots of the hotel in various decades (the building doesn't change, but the cars parked in front certainly do).

Rooms are small and, although simply furnished, feel more like a guest room in someone's house than in a hotel. The polished hardwood pine floors, soft blanket and soft white bedspread, the mahogany bureau with its own mirror, and the beveled mirror set in the closet door are all what you might find at home. Astonishingly, much of the furniture is actually the hotel's original furniture made by John Wannamaker in 1926. If you a want a little more space, ask for one of the several rooms with a king bed and an oversized bathroom.

The stairs are the quickest way to get to and from your room but for a bit of nostalgia take the ancient hand-operated elevator at least once. There's a tiny lobby bar and an adjoining veranda where guests gather each evening for cocktails and to solve the world's problems. Friday and Saturday nights, this lobby bar offers live entertainment. When the two of you are ready for the beach, you can walk five minutes to the public beach or drive two miles to the private Cabana Club, where you'll find the hotel's wonderful, heated, salt water pool and its own private beach and seasonal lunch restaurant.

Bar, hotel shops, putting green, saltwater pool (at Cabana Club). Smoke-free hotel. Hotel restaurant open for Continental breakfast. Check-out 11 a.m. 66 units. Owner/General Manager: Jestena Boughton. 525 East Atlantic Ave., Delray Beach, 33447. Res: 800.552.2363. Tel: 561.276.4123. Fax: 561.276.0123. Web: www.thecolonyhotel.com $59-$239

RESTAURANTS FOR LOVERS
AURA
For a truly romantic dinner, walk over to Aura. Its decor is subtle and yet dramatic. Stop for a drink at the long, dark bar and then head to the back of the restaurant where booths with high, curved backs create private spaces for romantic duos. Designer lamps give you just enough light to read the menu. Share a series of appetizers and a bottle of wine, or choose from a dazzling array of appealing entrees, such as Creole BBQ shrimp and Chile-Trinity rice, duck pappardelle, or pomegranate-molasses pork chops. *Dinner nightly. 290 E. Atlantic Ave., 561.243.2686 $$*

CAFE CIA TOTO
When you're both in the mood for some superb Italian cuisine day or night, just walk across the street to this inviting and intimate bistro. Choose a table on the sidewalk or a quieter one inside, where little square tables are draped in white under lazy ceiling fans. Listen carefully as the waiters describe the specials in thick Italian accents. Soup lovers will definitely want to start with the hearty pasta e fagioli. Good dinner choices include angel hair with a light tomato sauce, penne alle vodka, linguini with clams in a red or white sauce, veal chop in a gorgonzola-champagne sauce, and red snapper with white wine, tomatoes, capers, onions, and olives. This is also a wonderful place to come for a romantic lunch—try the shrimp Caesar or the lasagna with a glass of Pinot Grigio. *Dinner nightly, lunch Tues.-Sun. 522 E. Atlantic Ave., 561.278.3837 $$*

ROMANTIC THINGS TO DO HERE
Hold hands together and amble. East Atlantic Avenue is a tree-lined street with blocks of restaurants, bars, shops, boutiques, cafes, and art galleries. Wander along, stopping at whatever grabs your fancy. Eateries vary from casual to fancy and you can find just about anything you might want: pasta, sushi, an oyster bar, fresh seafood, inspired contemporary cuisine, burgers, grilled steaks, Irish pub fare.

When you want to be where everyone else is, come to Sopra (*110 E. Atlantic Ave., 561.274.7077*), Delray Beach's hottest restaurant, and mingle with the crowd at the bar.

61

Dine romantically at old-fashioned and elegant Vitorio's *(25 6th Ave. S., 561.278.5525)*. "Food with a touch of love" is the motto. Cuisine is classic Italian and dinner is served nightly except Tuesday.

Have lunch or dinner at the Blue Anchor *(804 E. Atlantic Ave., 561.272.7272)*. This pub was actually the Blue Anchor Pub in England for 150 years (Winston Churchill used to stop by to have a pint when he was a Fleet Street journalist) before it was brought over here.

For some really original retro items head to Pre-View *(11 S.E. 6th Ave., 561.276.8282)*. You'll find lamps, coffee tables, chairs, photographs, and objet d'art straight out of the 1940's to 1970's.

Enjoy an elegant and romantic French repast at La Belle Epoque *(253 S.E. 5th Ave., 561.272.5800)*, with its signature blue glassware and walls hung with paintings. It's a very short drive away.

Walk over to Old School Square *(corner of Swinton and E. Atlantic Ave., 561.243.7922)* and check out the exhibits at the Cornell Museum of Art & History and see who or what is playing at the Crest Theater (it could be jazz or a music fest or a new play).

Sip a classic cocktail at Dakotah 624's Martini Bar *(270 E. Atlantic Ave., 561.274.6244)* when you want to be part of a crowd.

Have lunch on the cool and breezy deck overlooking the waterway at Busch's Seafood Restaurant *(840 E. Atlantic Ave., 561.278.7600)*. Return at night for a delicious dinner and the evening singer.

Drive to the Morikami Park and Museum *(400 Morikami Park Rd., 561.495.0233)* and wander through these quiet Japanese gardens.

ROMANTIC RADIO
Easy: LOVE93.9FM Swing/jazz: WDBF1420AM Country: 107.9FM

HELPFUL HINTS: You'll want a beach cover-up for lunch at the Cabana Club. Delray is a late night town so plan to stay up and have fun.

Directions: I-95, exit 52. East on Rt. 806, which is Atlantic Ave.

ROMANTIC SUGGESTIONS

Laugh. Be silly. Tickle each other. Tell jokes. Hide behind a curtain and scare your partner. Be kids together. Find the child inside you.

Be decadently lazy. Don't jog or run or play tennis or swim laps. Go back to bed after breakfast. Or stay there together until dusk.

Take pictures of the two of you. Bring a camera with a timer so you can take pictures of yourselves together: hugging, kissing, laughing, embracing, smiling.

Renew your vows on the beach at sunrise or sunset. This can often be done with very little advance notice. All you have to do is check the Yellow Pages listings under weddings.

Dine at odd times. Eat breakfast at 11 a.m. Lunch at 3 p.m. Dinner at midnight. Restaurants are different places when no one else is around. You have the room almost to yourselves and the moments feel delightfully "stolen."

Avoid the "shoulds." Anytime either of you feels that you "should" do something, just don't do it. On the other hand, don't miss the stuff you'll really wish you had done once you get back home.

Watch people rush back to work. If you are in a city, go to lunch late and linger. Savor watching everyone else head back to work while you enjoy your freedom.

SO YOU WANT TO BE AN INNKEEPER?

Many people dream about completely changing their lives: picking up, packing up, and opening a Bed & Breakfast. Becoming innkeepers can sound so romantic.

A small number of people actually go for it each year. For some, it is a wonderfully romantic dream fulfilled; for others, a nightmare of monumental proportions.

If you have any serious thoughts about really exploring the possibility of owning a B&B, you would do well to invest the time and money and attend a "How to Acquire and Start Up a Bed & Breakfast" seminar. These excellent classes are run by David Caples, an experienced innkeeper, and are offered six or seven times a year.

These weekends are extremely informative and can add reality to the romance associated with owning a Bed & Breakfast. Seminars generally run Friday afternoon to Sunday afternoon and include lodging, most meals, and lots of input from professionals that will help you really decide if you want to become innkeepers or just continue dreaming about it.

For seminar dates, course descriptions, and prices, contact LodgingResources.com Workshops, 98 S. Fletcher Ave., Amelia Island, FL 32034. Tel: 888.201.7603 or 904.277.4851. Fax: 904.277.6500. Web: www.lodgingresources.com.

CHAPTER 12

A ROMANTIC ESCAPE TO FORT LAUDERDALE

AN OVERVIEW

A huge number of restaurants, outdoor cafes, art galleries, and clothing boutiques are squeezed into a pulsating, six-block-long strip of Las Olas Boulevard, several miles inland from the beach. Sidewalks are crowded day and night and the atmosphere is frenetic and electric.

If there's a bit of the salsa beat in the romantic throb of your heart, then for a lovers' escape you can't top the combination of Fort Lauderdale and the newly-expanded Riverside Hotel. It's sexy (there are giant mirrors over some of the beds) and it's a peaceful hideaway, but when the two of you want to be where everyone else is, just step out the door.

If you like to be alone in a crowd, you can head to the outdoor cafes but you can also always find a dark romantic corner inside restaurants if you prefer. To roam further, go out the hotel's rear entrance and catch a water bus, which travels the canals to a huge number of restaurants, museums, shopping areas, and even the beach.

LODGING FOR LOVERS
RIVERSIDE HOTEL

Lions flank the front entrance of this charming, intimate, and newly-expanded historic hotel which is right on trendy Las Olas Boulevard and is a quiet retreat from the "happening" atmosphere outside.

Two restaurants, room service, a newsstand, and a pool mean you never have to leave this full-service hotel. But when the two of you want to mingle with the crowds, find outdoor cafes, or look for late night entertainment, all you have to do is walk out to Las Olas Boulevard. If you want to venture further, say to the beach, just catch a water bus behind the hotel.

A new tower has doubled the number of rooms in the hotel and dramatically expanded the room choices. If you want a spacious room in the sky, with a contemporary bathroom and outstanding views of the city, boats and canals, and even the distant cruise ship docks, choose a tower room. If your preference is for a room out of an earlier era, then the rooms in the original building, built in 1936, are for you. The most romantic of these are the Canopy-King rooms with canopied beds and mirrored ceilings. Although quite small, rich dark fabrics make them cozy. Bathrooms have been remodeled but are still also a bit small. Some rooms and suites in the original building have balconies and views of Las Olas Boulevard or the waterway. All units in the hotel are tastefully decorated and have little refrigerators.

Downstairs, the Golden Lyon Lounge is a quiet spot for a drink (except during the bustling happy hour). For lunch or dinner, Indigo serves Southeast Asian and Indonesian cuisine outdoors and in (the quietest, most romantic table is inside by the fireplace). The Grill Room is the romantic place for dinner. In the afternoon, the two of you can order Royal Tea, an extravaganza that includes port wine and champagne. It's served in the gracious lobby by the fireplace.

2 restaurants, bar, room service 7 a.m.-10 p.m., pool. Non-smoking rooms available. Check-out 11 a.m. 221 rooms and suites. 620 East Las Olas Blvd., Fort Lauderdale, 33301. Res: 800.325.3280. Tel: 954.467.0671. Fax: 954.462.2148. Web: www.riversidehotel.com $119-$219 plus $10 parking

RESTAURANTS FOR LOVERS

Restaurants on Las Olas offer outdoor seating but the traffic noise can be jarring and generally the indoors is quieter and more romantic.

GRILL ROOM ON LAS OLAS
This dark and captivating restaurant combines couches and chairs for intimate seating arrangements. Settle in and be prepared for a world-class dining experience with excellent service. If you want, share everything: the Caesar salad prepared tableside, the chateaubriand carved tableside or the roast rack of lamb (both excellent with a side order of caramelized onions and mushrooms), and a bottle of red from the extensive wine list. The mostly Continental menu includes a wide selection of steaks (filet, strip, rib), plus roasted duck, sesame-seared tuna, and pumpkin-crusted snapper. There's a martini menu, oysters and caviar on the appetizer menu, and a stunning wine room. *Dinner nightly. 620 E. Las Olas Blvd., 954.467.0671 $$-$$$*

LAS OLAS CAFE
This quiet, hidden-away cafe just steps back from Las Olas Boulevard is indeed romantic, especially outdoors. Follow the walkway to the secluded courtyard and dine outside under the stars (there's also an intimate little indoor dining room). The cuisine is creative and superbly prepared. Try the shrimp stuffed with mozzarella or the crab spring rolls or the retro apple and walnut salad for a start, and then move on to walnut-crusted fresh fish or blackened shrimp or pasta Andre—penne pasta with spinach, wild mushrooms, and sun-dried tomatoes. *Dinner nightly. 922 E. Las Olas Blvd., 954.524.4300 $$*

LE CAFE DE PARIS
Inside this quiet and very French restaurant, it's peaceful, intimate, and delightfully dark. There are meals to share: Steak Diane and Filet au Poivre Flambe au Cognac are prepared at your table and a wonderful section of the menu is devoted to Celebration Dinners for Two. These include wine or champagne, Caesar salad for two, a selection of entrees to share (the Beef Wellington and Veal Cordon Bleu are superb), and a scrumptious Baked Alaska for Two. Other house favorites are bouillabaisse, shrimp scampi, and duck. *Dinner nightly, lunch Mon.-Sat. 715 E. Las Olas Blvd., 954.467.2900 $$$*

ROMANTIC THINGS TO DO HERE

Spend an evening enjoying fine French cuisine at the French Quarter *(215 S.E. 8th Ave., 954.463.8000)*. They have a wonderful keyboard player who entertains Wednesdays through Saturdays. This is a romantic lunching tryst, too.

Enjoy an old-fashioned carriage ride along the avenue. Call Royal Horse Drawn Carriages *(954.971.9820)*. You can also arrange to have them take you to dinner or pick you up for a romantic after-dinner ride.

For the trendiest restaurant decor and cuisine, don't miss stunning Mark's Las Olas *(1032 E. Las Olas Blvd., 954.463.1000)*. This is the place to be seen. At least stop by for a drink. For dinner, it's best to make reservations.

Hold hands and browse up and down the boulevard. Check out the appealing shops and galleries, stopping for a snack or a drink at an outside cafe, or you can just enjoy the sounds, sights, and people-watching that are all around you.

Find something fun to take home at Elements *(1034 Las Olas Blvd., 954.525.5754)* **and Seldom Seen** *(817 Las Olas Blvd., 954.764.5590)*. These shops are chock full of one-of-a-kind pieces of artwork, clocks, pottery, posters, furniture, cards, glassware, and wearable art. The more you look, the more you'll see.

Cruise five-and-a-half miles of waterway, stopping at shops, museums, and restaurants or just enjoying the sights. Catch the Water Bus *(954.467.6677)* right behind the hotel.

ROMANTIC RADIO
Easy: 93.9FM Classical: 93.1FM '70s-'80s: 97.3FM

HELPFUL HINTS: The dress code here seems to be either very casual or really hot casual. If you have a flashy, outrageous outfit, this is the place to wear it.

Directions: I-95, exit 27. East on Broward Blvd. to S.E. 8th Ave. Go right (south) to S.E. 4th (crossing Las Olas Blvd.). Turn right to hotel entrance.

WATCH OUT!

Following are some of the less wonderful things Florida offers that you might want to "watch out" for, a few things that might reduce the romance of your escape.

JACK SPANIELS. No they're not dogs; they're colorful insects that look a bit like wasps. They also sting like wasps.

GOAT'S HEADS OR SAND SPURS. These little spiked balls can turn up anywhere, from the path through the dunes to the beach, to a grassy area of a park. It is a good idea to wear something on your feet. You'll avoid the pain and bouncing around on one foot trying to extract these stinkers.

SHIRTS AND SHOES. Speaking of shoes, Florida law requires that you wear shirts and shoes in restaurants, bars, and stores that sell food so, if you're going to walk on a beach to "civilization" remember to bring flip-flops and a top.

FIRE ANTS. These little devils did not get their name by working for the local fire department. The safest way to avoid their fire-like sting is to avoid anything that looks like an ant when you are outside.

THUNDERSTORMS. They are romantic and magnificent to watch. Do this from inside. You are in the lightning capital of the country. And lightning is a killer.

THE DRIVERS. Florida has a volatile combination of retired people in no hurry to go anywhere, locals who are always in a hurry to get somewhere, and tourists who don't know where they're going anyway. Drive defensively so you'll be able to enjoy more romantic escapes in the future.

WHAT DO YOU WANT?

When you already have certain criteria for your romantic escape, you can use this chart to identify the properties that fit what you want.

RIGHT ON THE BEACH
Harrington House
Inn at Cocoa Beach
Lodge & Club at Ponte Vedra Beach
Palm Island Resort
Ritz-Carlton Amelia Island
Song of the Sea

ANTIQUES
Fort Lauderdale
Mount Dora
Naples
Palm Beach
St. Augustine
Winter Park

RESTAURANTS AND BARS WITHIN AN EASY WALK
Casa Monica Hotel
Celebration Hotel
Chesterfield Hotel
Colony Hotel & Cabana Club, Delray Beach
Colony Hotel, Palm Beach
Fairbanks House
Lakeside Inn
Live Oak Inn
Park Plaza Hotel
Riverview Hotel
Riverside Hotel
Song of the Sea

LAKE/RIVERFRONT
Celebration Hotel
Lakeside Inn
Turtle Beach Resort

24-HOUR ROOM SERVICE
Chesterfield Hotel
Lodge & Club at Ponte Vedra Beach
Peabody Orlando Hotel
Naples Registry Resort
Ritz-Carlton Amelia Island

WORKING FIREPLACES IN SOME ROOMS
Fairbanks House (electric)
Governors Inn
Harrington House
Inn at Cocoa Beach
Josephine's
Lodge & Club at Ponte Vedra Beach
BIKING
Amelia Island
Anna Maria Island
Celebration
Knight's Island
Mount Dora
New Smyrna Beach
KITCHENS AVAILABLE IN ROOMS
Palm Island Resort
Song of the Sea
Turtle Beach Resort
ART GALLERIES AND MUSEUMS
Delray Beach
Fort Lauderdale
Orlando
New Smyrna Beach
Palm Beach
St. Augustine
Winter Park
PLACES YOU DON'T REALLY NEED A CAR
Casa Monica Hotel
Celebration Hotel
Chalet Suzanne
Chesterfield Hotel
Colony Hotel & Cabana Club, Delray Beach
Colony Hotel, Palm Beach
Fairbanks House
Lakeside Inn
Lodge & Club at Ponte Vedra Beach
Palm Island Resort
Park Plaza Hotel
Peabody Orlando Hotel
Riverside Hotel
Ritz-Carlton Amelia Island

I Don't Know Much

We don't know much... and the pace of "everyday life" doesn't give us much luxury time to laze about and think about living and loving and how lucky we are. Make time on your next escape.

"I don't know much, but I know I love you, and that may be all I need to know." —*Aaron Neville*

"They talk about the dignity of work. Bosh. The dignity is in leisure." —*Melville*

"The way to love anything is to realize that it might be lost." —*Chesterton*

"A true relationship between a man and a woman is one in which the independence is equal, the dependence mutual, and the obligation reciprocal." —*Louis Anspacher*

"Today is unique, share it, do something wonderful with it . . . for it will never come again." —*Flavia*

"Love does not only exist in gazing at each other but in looking outward together in the same direction." —*Antoine de Saint-Exupery*

"The most thoroughly wasted of all days is that on which one has not laughed." —*Chamfort*

"One word frees us from all the weight and pain of life: That word is love." —*Sophocles*

SECTION 2

FLORIDA'S ROMANTIC INLAND

**TALLAHASSEE
MOUNT DORA
WINTER PARK
ORLANDO
CELEBRATION
LAKE WALES**

◆ROMANTIC
INLAND DESTINATIONS

GEORGIA

ATLANTIC
OCEAN

◆ Tallahassee

Mount Dora ◆

Winter Park ◆
◆ Orlando
Celebration ◆

◆
Lake Wales

GULF
OF
MEXICO

CHAPTER 13

A ROMANTIC ESCAPE TO TALLAHASSEE

AN OVERVIEW

The Tallahassee area is hilly and forested with fragrant pines. This quiet and dignified town in north Florida is the state's capital and the architecture in the Capitol Complex spans the centuries. Part of the Old Capitol was built before the Civil War but standing behind it is the New Capitol, a sleek 22-story skyscraper. Ancient oaks line many avenues and the parks are stunning in the spring when the azaleas are in bloom.

The charming Governors Inn is a comfortable and refined retreat just one block from the Capitol Complex. The two of you can settle in to a suite with a sleeping loft or a jetted tub. It can get chilly here in the winter and a suite with a fireplace (they supply the wood) is a warm winter choice.

An excellent restaurant and great jazz are right across the street and historical sights are nearby. There is no pool here and this definitely isn't a beach destination. However, the hilly streets and grassy parks are pleasant for quiet walks and romantic talks.

LODGING FOR LOVERS
THE GOVERNORS INN

Suites in this intimate and elegant inn are inviting and sophisticated quarters made for relaxing, sleeping, and taking it easy. A romantic restaurant is across the street.

A lovely brick walkway leads to the etched glass and varnished wood doors of this elegant inn. This building was originally a 19th-century hardware store, and the architect kept the handsome exterior brick and did a fine job of incorporating the original and massive heart-of-pine beams into a country French interior.

Each room and suite is named for a different governor of Florida and each is uniquely decorated. All are handsomely furnished with a mix of antiques and reproductions—four-poster beds, writing desks, armoires. You'll find thick terry robes in the closet and your shoes shined if you leave them outside the door when you retire.

The standard rooms are on the small side, but the appealing furnishings make them cozy and inviting retreats. However, the unusual suites are the real romantic draw here. No two are alike in shape or size. In the suites you'll find sky-lights, high ceilings, and charming little windows. Some have wood-burning marble fireplaces and circular stairways that lead up to a romantic loft bedroom. One unit has a sexy whirlpool tub. These suites are comfortable and well-appointed and inviting places to settle into.

Groupings of upholstered chairs and sofas are scattered around the spacious and warm, pine-paneled Florida Room. Guests gather here for complimentary cocktails in the early evening. Continental breakfast is served here in the morning, but it's much more romantic to call down and have them bring it to your room so you can enjoy it in bed. Restaurants are a short walk away.

During the weekdays transportation from the airport is provided. Non-smoking rooms available. Check-out noon. 40 rooms and suites. 209 S. Adams St., Tallahassee, 32301. Res: 800.342.7717. Tel: 850.681.6855. Fax: 850.222.3105. $129-$229

A RESTAURANT FOR LOVERS
ANDREW'S 228

The Mediterranean decor in this hip, urban, and very classy and romantic restaurant is reminiscent of a Tuscan villa. The enticing menu features a delightful blend of contemporary, Italian, and true steakhouse favorites Come here for mussels in garlic broth, ciopinno, panko-crusted halibut on grilled romaine, rack of lamb with crispy white bean ravioli, and peppercorn crusted N.Y. strip. *Dinner nightly. 228 S. Adams St., 850.222.3444 $$-$$$*

ROMANTIC THINGS TO DO HERE

In the spring when the azaleas are in bloom, don't miss the stunning 307-acre Maclay Ornamental Gardens *(3540 Thomasville Rd., 850.487.4556)*. Come for hiking, biking, and horseback riding.

Head to the LeMoyne Art Center *(125 N. Gadsen St., 850.222.8800)* for the current exhibit, the sculpture garden, and classical music.

Enjoy a casual drink, a burger, or a hearty steak at Andrew's Capital Grill and Bar *(228 S. Adams St., 850.222.3444)*.

Dine romantically inside a restored 1920s house or outside under the oaks and enjoy superbly-prepared French cuisine at Chez Pierre *(1215 Thomasville Rd., 850.222.0936)*.

For a great and graciously-served Italian meal go straight to Anthony's *(1950 Thomasville Rd., 850.224.1447)*.

Catch a spectacular view of the city. Take an elevator to the 22nd floor observatory atop the Florida State Capitol at Monroe Street.

ROMANTIC RADIO
Soft rock: 98.9FM   Jazz: 100.9FM

HELPFUL HINTS: When the state house and senate are in session this area is bustling with politicians.

Directions: I-10, exit 199 (US 27). South on US 27 (Monroe) for seven mi. Right on Jefferson. Immediate right on Adams. The inn is halfway up the block.

PLAN YOUR ESCAPE...

A Magical Romantic Escape Doesn't Happen Like Magic

The truth is that whether you and your lover are escaping for a weekend or a few weeks, you have to do some work to make it work. Here are some planning hints to help you enjoy your escape a little bit more.

❑**Make sure you both agree on your "escape"** and choose your destination together. Make sure you both understand what there is to do there . . . and what there isn't.

❑**Remember that very few mortals can leave a hectic and high-pressured pace and just "decide" to be relaxed, romantic, and walk barefoot in the sand.** Try to plan something the day before you leave—an afternoon rest, or a leisurely dinner, or a long evening walk—to get the wind-down process started before you make your escape.

❑**Give yourself the gift of time**—plenty of time for an unhurried departure and plenty of travel time to get where you are going. And, of course, the time to do whatever the two of you want to do after you get there.

❑**You have the privilege of taking a special trip with the person you love very much.** The two of you belong to each other this trip. Not to the office, not to the kids, not to anyone but each other.

❑**Plan a "soft landing" for your return to "reality."** A dinner for two after you get home. The kids or phone calls or messages or mail or work can survive without you for another twelve hours or so.

CHAPTER 14

A ROMANTIC ESCAPE TO MOUNT DORA

AN OVERVIEW

You drive through fields and farm country to get to Mount Dora, a tiny lakeside town in central Florida. Orlando is only 45 minutes away, but you feel as if you are in the middle of nowhere. The scenery is beautiful here and also quite unlike most people's idea of Florida. The land is vaguely hilly and densely covered with leafy green trees.

Mount Dora's romantic hideaway is the Lakeside Inn, built in 1883 and listed on the National Register of Historic Places. It's right on a lake and if either of you has ever spent a summer by a lake anywhere, this lovely inn will strike a nostalgic chord.

Just around the corner from the inn is a charming little town with a large number of antique stores, several art galleries, and a collection of restaurants. You can walk everywhere along quiet, tree-lined streets. This is not a place to come for late night activities. Most restaurants close here by 9 p.m. during the week, somewhat later on weekends. When you tire of walking the town, there are boat trips to catch your fancy.

LODGING FOR LOVERS
THE LAKESIDE INN

Built in 1883 and overlooking a peaceful lake where you can canoe or take a boat ride, this nostalgic inn has a picturesque little town right around the corner and it's just a short walk to interesting antique shops and art galleries and a fine choice of restaurants.

Your grandparents or great-grandparents may have actually stayed here if they vacationed in Florida. White wicker rocking chairs line the inn's long veranda and a green lawn sweeps down to the large pool and serene Lake Dora. At sunset the lake reflects the spectacular colors of the evening sky and at night it catches the stars.

The rooms are in a cluster of wooden buildings which resemble oversized houses, painted pale yellow with steep gables and green-shingled roofs. Each of the 88 rooms is a slightly different shape and size. All have wonderfully high ceilings, are nicely painted or wallpapered, and have large closets (for those trunks full of fancy attire guests traveled with in the 1920s, when the inn was in its heyday). Hallways creak here and bathrooms are comfortably old-fashioned.

The most romantic rooms are probably the extra-large lakefront rooms with giant picture windows that frame the water view, but it's also romantic to stay on the second floor of the main building. Lake views here are further away but still good, and you can just walk downstairs to meals and the inn's large, inviting living room with a fireplace. For a romantic splurge, go for the private third-floor suite with a living room and bedroom, both with superb views of the lake.

The Beauclaire Dining Room is open for all meals plus brunch on Sunday and there is room service during regular meal hours. Tremain's Lounge has lively entertainment on weekends.

Restaurant, bar, room service during meal hours, pool, tennis courts, horseshoes, shuffleboard, croquet. Fee for canoes, boats, bikes, cruises. Some rooms with refrigerators. Non-smoking rooms available. Check-out 11 a.m. 88 rooms. 100 N. Alexander St., Mount Dora, 32757. Res: 800.556.5016. Tel: 352.383.4101. Fax: 352.735.2642. Web: www.lakeside-inn.com $90-$150

A RESTAURANT FOR LOVERS
GOBLIN MARKET
The romantic setting here is the first floor of a quaint frame house. Tables are well-spaced in two dark and intimate rooms. Papered walls and shelves of books provide a cozy background for a long and splendid evening. The menu is eclectic and inventive. Try the crab bisque, or the escargot, or the wild mushroom tartare for starters. Then opt for the porcini-dusted veal, or the bourbon-glazed pork tenderloin, or the snapper seared with a caramelized onion crust. When the weather is agreeable, the outside courtyard in back is a romantic choice. Come Thursday to hear a gifted acoustic guitar player. *Reservations necessary. Dinner Tues.-Sat. 331-B Donnelly St., 352.735.0059 $$-$$$*

ROMANTIC THINGS TO DO HERE
Stroll out to the end of the spacious dock at night. You'll hear loons, see a zillion stars, frequently catch spectacular thunderstorm light shows in the distance and sparkling firefly shows up close.

See if you can spot an alligator after dark. Romantic? Well, you have to do it together in the dark. Walk out to the end of the dock and look for a silent, slightly darker shape gliding silently in the still water. Shine a flashlight to see if it's a gator. It's a little scary when you make contact with those red eyes.

Step up and hop into an old-fashioned horse-drawn carriage. Call Classic Carriages (*352.589.2555*) and take a romantic ride through downtown Mount Dora.

Get a table for two and share a special "dinner for two" at the casual Palm Tree Grill (*351 Donnelly St., 352.735.1936*). Choose between a sumptuous platter of shrimp scampi, lobster tail, and N.Y. strip or a seafood extravaganza. Or order separately and dine on some excellent Italian food.

Have a cafe au lait and browse through the many books at the inviting Dickens-Reed (*140 W. 5th St., 352.735.5950*) bookstore. Check their schedule for upcoming events.

81

Go to a play together at the Ice House Theater (*1100 N. Unser St., 352.383.4616*). There's a play every month except July and August.

For a taste of Britain, drop by the Windsor Rose English Tea Room (*144 W. 4th Ave., 352.735.2551*) for authentic scones and pastries and also excellent sandwiches.

Head out to a winery for a tasting. Lakeridge Winery & Vineyards (*19239 US 27N., 352.394.8627*) in Clarmont is a pretty 45-minute drive away on winding roads around lakes and over small hills.

Spend the morning putt-putting around the lake in your own little run-about. Call Fun Boats (*Lakeside Inn, 352.735.2669*) to rent powerboats, pontoon boats, paddle boats, canoes, and chairboats. You can even boat over to an Irish pub, O'Keefe's (*352.343.2157*), and have lunch.

Have fun sampling the wines at Shiraz (*301 Baker St., 352.735.5227*) any day. Stay for dinner Wednesday through Saturday.

Go antiquing. Pick up a map of the village at the Chamber of Commerce (*341 Alexander St., 352.383.2165*) or just start walking. You'll find one great shop after another.

Go on a cruise around Lake Dora. Check with Fun Boats (*Lakeside Inn, 352.735.2669*). They take a maximum of six at a time on one- and two-hour pontoon boat cruises.

ROMANTIC RADIO
Easy: 107.7FM   Oldies: 105.9FM

HELPFUL HINTS: Mount Dora is a popular day trip destination on weekends and the streets can get crowded midday on Saturday and Sunday. The town also hosts many special weekend events. If you want to attend an event or escape the crowds, call the very helpful Chamber of Commerce (*352.383.2165*) to find out what will or won't be happening when you plan to visit.

Directions: 35 mi. northwest of Orlando, off of Rt. 441. The Lakeside Inn provides excellent driving directions.

A VERY SPECIAL FLORIDAY

FRESH ORANGE JUICE IN BED
OR ON THE BEACH

A MORNING STROLL ARM IN ARM

SOME SHOPPING OR SNOOZING IN THE
MORNING SUN

A BACK RUB AND A BATH

A PICNIC IN THE PINES - A LOAF OF BREAD,
JUG OF WINE, AND THOU

SOME SPLENDOR IN THE GRASS

AN AFTERNOON DIP

AN ICE CREAM CONE OR TWO

SOME BUBBLY IN A BUBBLE BATH

SOME FINE FOOD AND FLICKERING LIGHT

A DANCE AROUND THE FLOOR

THEN TUCKED IN BED TOGETHER
FOR THE NIGHT

Inexpensive Romantic Gifts

Wine — You can find terrific wines in bottles and half-bottles for under ten dollars; if you aren't sure what to buy, ask the salesperson for assistance.

Flowers — Buy cut flowers by the stem, rather than in an arrangement, and you'll save quite a bit of money. Or just get one exquisite flower: a perfect rose or a fancy lily.

A Picture Frame — You can buy a fine-looking one in a K-Mart or a Walgreens's for just a few dollars. Add a special snapshot and it becomes a priceless gift.

Bath salts or bubble bath — Pick up some of this wonderful inexpensive gift you can enjoy together.

Candles — You can buy candles almost anywhere, and there are usually some on sale. Candles add immediate romance to a dinner or bath or even a midnight snack.

Books — All bookstores have bargain tables where you can purchase great books for a fraction of the original price. Find a book of scenic photographs or a book on a hobby or sport you both share.

Candy — You don't need a box of Godiva chocolate that takes two people to lift to show that you're sweet on your lover.

CHAPTER 15

A ROMANTIC ESCAPE TO WINTER PARK

AN OVERVIEW

In central Florida, just a few minutes northwest of downtown Orlando is the little college town of Winter Park, a peaceful enclave where the boughs of century-old oaks form canopies across quiet streets. Shops, art galleries, restaurants, and even a wonderful museum are on calm Park Avenue, a brick drive that runs alongside a lovely park. Even more restaurants and shops are just a few blocks away.

The most romantic lodging choice in Winter Park is the Park Plaza Hotel. This restored inn adjoins one of the most romantic restaurants in town, and it is right on Park Avenue.

It's the whole relaxing experience, not so much the bits and pieces, that make it romantic to escape to Winter Park. The center of town is quiet and everything to see and do is within an easy walking distance or is just an easy drive away. Walk around the college campus. Sit in the park and watch the birds. Browse in the shops. Stop at an outdoor cafe for a casual lunch or an evening beverage.

LODGING FOR LOVERS
PARK PLAZA HOTEL

Built in the 1920s, this renovated two-story cross between a hotel and an inn is a comfortable and romantic spot to settle into. It is just steps away from restaurants, cafes, shops, and the peaceful park.

A profusion of tropical plants and flowers fill the wrap-around second-floor balcony. Individually decorated rooms have richly patterned wallpapers, fancy moldings, oriental rugs, and hardwood floors. The smaller rooms are cozily romantic but if you plan to spend some time inside, you'll probably want a Balcony Suite which comes with a king bed and a living room area plus a door to the balcony.

Order up the complimentary continental breakfast for two and enjoy it in bed or out on the little balcony (although it's communal, the plants keep most tables private). In winter, during a cold snap, sit by the fire in the lobby or stay under the covers and share a bottle of champagne. For a romantic restaurant, just walk downstairs to the Park Plaza Gardens for lunch or dinner or a great Sunday brunch (or have a romantic meal in your room—this restaurant provides room and bar service for the hotel from 11 a.m. to 11 p.m.).

Non-smoking rooms available. No children under 5. Check-out noon. Proprietor: Sandra C. Spang. 27 rooms and suites. 307 S. Park Ave., Winter Park, 32789. Res: 800.228.7220. Tel: 407.647.1072. Fax: 407.647.4081. Web: www.parkplazahotel.com $95-$225

If you want to stay at a place with a pool . . .
BEST WESTERN MOUNT VERNON INN

Why a Best Western in a book on romance? Well, this two-story motel was built a long time ago and rooms are larger than you would expect to find in a motel. Also, although the front entrance is off of busy, four-lane US 17-92, it is easy to drive out the back onto a quiet road, and drive just several blocks to both Park Avenue and Winter Park Village. Many rooms are built around a courtyard and these rooms are particularly quiet and good for sleeping. The staff here are very friendly and helpful. *Bar, pool. Non-smoking rooms available. Check-out 11 a.m. 143 rooms. 110 S. Orlando Ave., Winter Park, 32789. Res: 800.992.3379. Tel: 407.647.1166. Fax 407.647.8011. Web: www.bestwestern.com/mtvernoninn $89-$129*

RESTAURANTS FOR LOVERS
ALLEGRIA
Paintings on the stuccoed ochre and peach walls, decorative tiles on the floor, and crisp table linens provide a romantic background for a memorable lunch or dinner. The creative Italian menu includes such delights as broccoli rabe and sausage, polenta quattro formaggi, and field greens with seared scallops for starters, and for the main course, lobster ravioli with truffle butter and sage, bucatini amatriciana with guanciale and pecorino, and veal saltimbocca. The long and elegant bar is an enjoyable spot to share a bottle of wine and perhaps a plate of antipasto from the delectable table display. *Dinner nightly, lunch Mon.-Sat. 115 E. Lyman Ave., 407.628.1641 $$-$$$*

PARK PLAZA GARDENS
This quiet, dimly-lit oasis is particularly romantic at night. Tiny white lights twinkle in the boughs of full-size potted trees and the atmosphere is peaceful, refined, and never hurried. For a tasty beginning, try the daily risotto special or the five-onion soup. Then move on to the crab cake with potato puree and corn salsa, the herb-seared N.Y. strip, or the black grouper with roasted peppers. A pianist plays during dinner on weekends and during brunch on Sunday. *Dinner Tues.-Sun., lunch Tues.-Sat., Sun. brunch. 319 S. Park Ave., 407.645.2475 $$$*

ROMANTIC THINGS YOU CAN WALK TO
To see enormous, beautifully romantic Tiffany glass murals and to read what must be the most delightfully amusing descriptive captions ever written, go to the Morse Museum (*445 N. Park Ave., 407.645.5311*). Do walk through Tiffany's stunning 1893 chapel interior, painstakingly reassembled here, and an awesome sight.

Check out Timothy's Gallery (*212 N. Park Ave., 407.629.0707*) for blown glass, tiles by Sophie, handcrafted jewelry, and colorful tables.

Walk to a boat trip around Lake Osceola with Winter Park Scenic Boat Tours (*Morse Blvd. at Lake Osceola, 407.644.4056*).

If you fell in love in college, let a walk through the Rollins College campus stir up romantic memories. Go to a play, a concert, or a game.

Hear Michael Lamy croon Broadway show songs and play the piano at the Village Bistro *(326 S. Park Ave., 407.740.7573)* on weekends.

Browse the Nicole Miller boutique *(312 Park Ave., 407.628.0400)* for sexy cocktail dresses and wonderfully zany neckties.

Take a look at the jewelry and watches at Reynolds and Company Jewelers *(232 Park Ave., 407.645.-2278)*. If you're in the market for something fancy at a great price, ask to see the estate watch selection.

Lunch on superbly fresh fixin's at the casual Powerhouse Cafe *(111 E. Lyman Ave., 407.645.3616)*. Try the delicious fruit smoothies, vegetarian sandwiches, fresh salads, and the tasty specialty, tuna salad with bulgar wheat tucked in a pita. Dine inside or take it to the park.

ROMANTIC STOPS A SHORT DRIVE AWAY
Spend some time day or night at the very nearby Winter Park Village *(Park Ave. to west on Canton Ave., then last right before US17-92, between Albertson's and Owen's Allen)*, where crowds head to dine at the ever popular Brio Tuscan Grill. You'll also find Ruth's Chris Steak House, P. F. Chang's, and the Black Fin plus movies, Borders, Pier One, and specialty stores.

For a superb lunch or dinner go straight to stylish Antonio's *(611 S. Orlando Ave., 407.645.5523)*. It's a five-minute drive and the cuisine is pure Italian, from the bufala mozzarella to the linguini alle vongole.

Enjoy a decadent dessert, or light cuisine, or just a glass of wine, and see award-winning movies at the Enzian Theater *(1300 S. Orlando Ave., 407.629.1088)*.

ROMANTIC RADIO
Easy: 107.7FM   Jazz: 103.1FM   Oldies: 105.9FM

HELPFUL HINTS: Light sleepers can be bothered by the trains next to the Park Plaza Hotel and might prefer the Best Western Mount Vernon.

Directions: I-4, exit 88. East on Lee Rd. to US17-92 and turn right. Go to Webster St. (1st light) and go left. Go to Park Ave. and turn right.

Words of Wisdom

Specials on Hotel Rooms. Ask about them. Ask about resident specials, midweek specials, seasonal specials, AAA specials, romantic specials. You get the idea. From a resort hotel to a four-room Bed & Breakfast, there are often ways to stay there for substantially less than the printed rate.

Unpleasant Surprises. Avoid them. Ask if there are any unusual events taking place where you are going. You don't want to pick a sleepy, out-of-the-way escape and find out it is the one weekend in the entire year when they host a national rap music concert.

Getting There. As much as possible try to make getting to your escape part of the fun. Bring some of your favorite music or a book-on-tape or some of those old radio shows to play in the car. Or play one of those old-fashioned games like categories. If you get stuck in traffic, relax.

Take Good Care of Yourselves. If you forgot your toothbrush or you want more pillows or an extra blanket, call housekeeping or the front desk and ask. If you want your room made up at a certain time or a late check out, just ask.

©2003 by Pamela Acheson and Richard B. Myers from *The Best Romantic Escapes in Florida, Vol. One*

Money and Restaurants. You really can go to expensive restaurants even on a budget. Order a glass of house wine instead of a bottle, order one of the least expensive entrees, and skip dessert (or stop and get it on the way home). You'll be able to experience fine food, gracious service, and a romantic evening for maybe half of what the table next to you is paying.

Rewards Upon Arrival. Pack a mini cooler as a "welcome to your escape" reward. Champagne and caviar, milk and cookies, mixed nuts and some beer. It doesn't matter what. Sometimes you just want to veg out and snack while you unpack. If you're a bit lazy, you can arrange (for a price, of course) to have a cheese tray, or wine, or whatever waiting for you in your room.

Make Some Memories. Take some photographs. If you forgot your camera, buy a throw-away. Even if you end up throwing away the pictures. Take a camera.

Reservations and Restaurants. It's a good idea to make dinner reservations and when you do, tell them you are on a romantic escape and would like a romantic table.

Turn Off Your Cell Phone. Really. Leave the phone number of your hotel with a few key people in case of emergency only. You won't believe how relaxing it can be.

CHAPTER 16

A ROMANTIC ESCAPE TO ORLANDO

AN OVERVIEW

Located in the middle of the state, Orlando is a sprawling city criss-crossed by major highways. Thirty years ago Orlando didn't even have a proper airport but now, thanks to Mr. Disney and to the influx of corporate headquarters, it's an internationally known destination. Just south of downtown is a giant convention center and a number of business hotels, one of which is actually also delightfully romantic.

When the two of you want to retreat from the world and settle into a sophisticated full-service hotel that you don't have to leave, head to the Peabody Orlando hotel. There's a complete spa, a superbly romantic restaurant, an Olympic-size swimming pool plus places to bask in the sun or sit in the shade, a poolside snack bar, tennis courts, an Italian bistro, a '50s-style diner, a take-out deli, dancing, and three bars. It's close to Disney World but you'd never, ever know it.

If you do want to go off to see an Orlando Magic game or make a foray to Epcot (or even to see Mickey), the Peabody Orlando also makes a wonderfully romantic base for exploring Central Florida.

LODGING FOR LOVERS
THE PEABODY ORLANDO

Excellent service and two outstanding restaurants turn this posh high-rise hotel into a luxurious romantic hideaway.

This is a 27-story high-rise hotel with a lot of space around it and windows on the upper floors showcase the flat Florida landscape and spectacular lightning when a thunderstorm rolls in. Rooms are comfortable and decorated in soft restful colors. Executive King units have a spacious seating area.

You can keep the draperies drawn and stay in bed all day here, or you can head down to the lobby to shop, or out to the pool and tennis courts, or go sit at a bar. Mallard's is the bar just off the lobby and in the back, tucked in between the columns, are two hidden seating nooks. The smaller one is perfect for lovers. Capriccio's bar is intimate and usually peaceful and quiet. Dux has a tiny, elegant bar.

You can also settle into comfortable chairs in the atrium Lobby Bar and listen to a pianist during cocktail hour. Later in the evening, there's music and dancing. In the afternoon stop by for tea. The hotel's signature ducks come and go from the lobby fountain every day (there's a duck-marching ceremony at 11 a.m. and 5 p.m.).

Dining choices abound at the Peabody, where there's even an all-night diner. For a romantic evening, head down to award-winning Dux or to the more casual Capriccio, which specializes in northern Italian cuisine. For a delicious meal anytime day or night, get a table at the '50s-style B-Line Diner. It's open 24 hours and also has a take-out counter. The heated Olympic-size pool is in a large courtyard with shade trees and Coconuts Pool Bar. Various shops plus a Delta Airline and Avis Car Rental desk can be found in the lobby.

3 restaurants, 3 bars, snackbar, 24-hour room service, pool, health club, lighted tennis courts. Non-smoking rooms available. Check-out noon. 871 rooms. 9801 International Dr., Orlando, 32819. Res: 800-PEA-BODY. Tel: 407.352.4000. Fax: 407.363.1505. Web: www.peabodyorlando.com $295-$420 (many specials throughout the year at lower rates; inquire)

RESTAURANTS FOR LOVERS
DUX
All tables are romantic in this intimate, formal setting, but the most romantic seats are in the corners. The innovative menu changes seasonally but includes such creations as tempura-fried escargots, roast sea scallops, a warm Florida lobster and rock shrimp salad, monk fish osso bucco with pancetta, pan-seared medallions of venison with chive ravioli and a potato and black truffle torte, plus desserts such as warm chocolate cake or a port-poached pear. Jackets are required for men. *Dinner Mon.-Sat. 407.352.4000 ext. 4550 $$$*

CAPRICCIO
Dine lightly or have a multi-course meal at this delightful northern Italian trattoria. Start with a bottle of Pinot Grigio and a traditional Caesar salad and then order two crispy pizzas and share them both. Or try the angel hair with tomatoes, or the penne with portabello mushrooms and sun-dried tomatoes, or the veal marsala. It can be clattery close to the kitchen, so for a quiet table, ask to be near a window, where it's darker and more romantic. Reservations are a must for the sumptuous Sunday brunch. *Dinner Tues.-Sun., Sun. brunch. 407.352.4000 ext. 4450 $$*

ROMANTIC THINGS TO DO HERE
Relax together in a bubble bath. No, the tub isn't oversize, but two can fit and there's bath gel provided.

Pamper yourselves and spend a half-day together in the spa. Have deep-tissue Swedish or relaxation massages. Try an hour-and-a-half, or even two. If you want, a massage therapist will come to your room.

Shop for bathing suits next to the spa. The selections are superb.

ROMANTIC RADIO
Easy: 107.7FM   Oldies:105.9FM   Country: 97FM

HELPFUL HINTS: Bring dress-up clothes for Dux and catch the duck parade.

Directions: I-4, exit 72 to Beeline Expwy. Next exit north to International Dr.

93

ROMANTIC FLORIDA STUFF

Key Lime Pie

Spring Training

Small Friendly Towns

The Warmth

Water, Water Everywhere

The Seasons. Yes, The Seasons

A-1-A

The Natural Beauty

Biking

Mangroves

The Intracoastal Waterway

CHAPTER 17

A ROMANTIC ESCAPE TO CELEBRATION

AN OVERVIEW

Celebration is southwest of downtown Orlando and northeast of Disneyworld. It's a planned community, created by Disney, and designed to have all the best elements of an old-fashioned small town.

Celebration has the "picture-perfect" Disney touch, but indeed, the perfection is quite enviable. Lanes curve past pastel-painted houses with shiny tin roofs and beautifully manicured front lawns. The hub of Celebration is a peaceful town square, set along the north side of a lake. Families and couples stroll along wide sidewalks, stopping at restaurants or shops, going to the bank or the post office or into the movie theater. If only real life could be this serene, you might wonder.

Overlooking the lake and right in town is the nostalgic and romantic Celebration Hotel. Visiting Celebration is a one-of-a-kind romantic escape. The town is more "perfect" than a town developed over time ever could be and it's a kick to be here. It may not feel quite like reality, but it's a fabulous escape.

LODGING FOR LOVERS
CELEBRATION HOTEL

You leave the real world behind when you stay at this nostalgic and romantic lakeside inn, with an old-fashioned town square just outside.

This sprawling three-story hotel is right on a lake and imbued with the style of 1920s Florida. It's a frame structure with dormer windows, clapboard siding, and tin roofs. Inside wainscotting and brick continue the old-Florida theme. In the lobby, paddle ceiling fans turn lazily, and comfortable seating arrangements are well-spaced on the Brazilian walnut hardwood floors.

Almost all rooms and suites are on the second and third floors. They are painted pale yellow and furnished with handsome reproduction armoires and four-poster beds with big comforters to cuddle under. Many have balconies with stunning lake views.

The Plantation Room restaurant is open mornings and evenings. Lunch is served in the lobby lounge. Breakfast is an elegant affair, with linen tablecloths and fine settings. Choose your ingredients at the omelet stand (or ask for eggs any style) or just select from the expansive cold buffet. Come back for a romantic dinner *(see page 97)*. In the evening, guests gather around the lobby bar, with its stunning mural of Florida wildlife. Weekends, a pianist often entertains.

Sets of double doors open out from the lobby to a long veranda overlooking a peaceful lake. Settle into a rocking chair, or walk to the adjacent pool to have a swim and catch some sun, or head around to the private outdoor whirlpool with a view of the lake and sky or the stars after dark. When you feel like a stroll through town or around the lake, just head out the door. For a kick, ask the bellman to drive you around town or to dinner in the vintage 1948 Cadillac parked at the entrance. It's complimentary.

Restaurant, bar, room service 6 a.m.-11p.m, pool, exercise room. Golf, fitness nearby. Non-smoking rooms available. Check out 11 a.m. 115 units. 700 Bloom St., Celebration, 34747. Res: 888.499.3800. Tel: 407.566.6000. Fax: 407.566.1844. Web: www.celebrationhotel.com $185-$470 plus $5 resort fee

A RESTAURANT FOR LOVERS
CAFE D'ANTONIO'S

Dine outside looking across at the lake or choose a quiet inside corner table for a romantic repast. You may think you've somehow slipped into Italy, as the cuisine is authentic Italian and so are many of the charming waitstaff. Come here for classic dishes: pasta e fagioli, veal marsala, spaghetti bolognese and some fine Italian reds. *Lunch, dinner daily. 691 Front St., 407.566.2233 $$-$$$*

PLANTATION ROOM

The atmosphere is quiet and romantic in this elegant room with hardwood floors, paddle fans, and white table linens. The menu features fresh grouper, shrimp, grilled duck, and steak paired with southern favorites with a twist: sweet potato grits, BBQ glaze with cilanto, fried leeks. *Dinner Tues.-Sat., Sun. brunch. 700 Bloom St., 407.566.6000 $$-$$$*

ROMANTIC THINGS TO DO HERE

Take a carriage ride through town Friday or Saturday evening between 6 p.m. 10 p.m. Catch it across from Cafe D'Antonio's.

Follow the path that goes around the lake or across to another lake, stopping along the way at a bench to talk and take in the view.

Wander around town. Shop for a teddy bear, Tommy Bahama clothes, and Sherlock Holmes memorabilia, have coffee at Barnies, stop in a diner for mealoaf, or in an ice cream shop for a root beer float, or at the Columbia Restaurant for tapas and sangria, or go to a movie.

ROMANTIC RADIO
Jazz: 103.1FM Easy: 107.7FM Oldies: 105.9FM Country: 97FM

HELPFUL HINTS: Bear in mind that this is a family-oriented village and if there is an evening event for children, there might be many, many children around. Nostalgic northerners might want to know that it snows here every evening in December.

Directions: Toll Rd. 417, exit 2. Take Celebration Ave. to Sycamore St. Turn left. Drive to Front St. Turn right. Turn left at Bloom St.

WHAT IS THE AUTHORS' FAVORITE ESCAPE?

The inevitable question for us at any book signing or during any interview is: "Well, of all these destinations which is *your* favorite romantic escape?"

The answer is "All of the escapes in this book and its companion, *The Best Romantic Escapes in Florida, Volume Two,* are our favorites." That may sound like the politically correct answer, but it is also the truth.

Which escape becomes our "favorite" depends on what has been happening in our lives. If we've been chained to our desks for weeks dealing with deadlines, then a perfect romantic escape might be the elegant Chesterfield, with lots of restaurants and nightlife nearby. Or the Registry, where we can enjoy the beach, fine dining, be pampered at the Spa, and dance the night away at Club Zanzibar without leaving the property.

If we've just finished a six-week authors' tour and been in a different city every day, then the perfect romantic escape might be Turtle Beach Resort where we have our own hot tub and our own kitchen and can cook what we like or have a delicious meal delivered from Ophelia's. Or it might be Palm Island Resort where we can dine when we want and live in a bathing suit.

The point is that any couples' "perfect romantic escape" may be different from one month to the next. It is why this book gives you so many very different destinations that share one common ingredient: romance!

— *P.A. and R.B.M.*

CHAPTER 18

A ROMANTIC ESCAPE TO LAKE WALES

AN OVERVIEW

Lake Wales is pretty much in the center of central Florida. The town is well south of Disneyworld and in between Tampa to the west and Vero Beach to the east. Lake Wales is "out of the loop" in terms of the Interstates. Being there is close to really being absolutely in the middle of nowhere. The town itself is very tiny and there's not much to do (although there is now a small mall, some antique shops, and even a movie theater).

Outside of this town, and even more remote, is the incomparable Chalet Suzanne Restaurant and Country Inn. This historic inn is set in rolling countryside, along a tiny lake.

When the two of you want comfortable seclusion at a small inn in the country with formal dining, then Chalet Suzanne just might be the romantic choice. It's the perfect venue for a relaxing, indulgent, and romantic stay. Do nothing, or walk around the lake, or play croquet, or stay in bed all day. Bring books to read. This is one escape where you can really get away from it all.

LODGING FOR LOVERS
CHALET SUZANNE

Chalet Suzanne Restaurant & Country Inn is an extremely peaceful hideout for lovers. You can relax and do nothing in comfort. It's refined, eclectic, and yet ever-so-slightly whimsical.

This celebrated inn is on a 70-acre estate with neatly manicured grounds, a small lake, and its very own little grass airstrip. Thirty unique rooms are clustered together in an architectural jumble of spires and steeples, little balconies, gabled roofs, and arched doorways. It may sound odd, but it works.

Rooms come in all sizes and shapes and are individually decorated with a mix of antique and reproduction furniture, photographs and paintings, porcelain figurines, old clocks, and fresh flowers. A dumbwaiter runs to the honeymoon suite so meals can be delivered without disturbing the newlyweds. *Select Request* rooms (the most expensive category) have larger sitting areas, have been upgraded, and have jetted tubs and king beds.

For such a little place, there are a number of diversions. You can swim in the pool, laze in the sun, read in the shade, look for rabbits on the lawn and turtles in the lake, wander through the tiny antique shop (only items with price tags are actually for sale), buy a ceramic dish from a resident ceramic artist, have your very own tile made for the autograph garden, or browse in the little gift shop. Golf, tennis, sky-diving, and therapeutic massage can be arranged.

Be sure to stop by the delightful soup "factory" and ask someone to show you around. This is the home of the Chalet Suzanne soups sold in gourmet shops worldwide and the improbable setup of the quaint cooking and canning apparatus is unlike anything you have ever seen.

Restaurant, bar, pool, croquet, horseshoes, antique shop, ceramic shop, gift shop. Non-smoking rooms available. Check-out noon. 30 units. Innkeepers: Henshaw family. 3800 Chalet Suzanne Dr., Lake Wales, 33859. Res: 800.433.6011. Tel: 863.676.6011. Fax: 863.676.1814. Web: www.chaletsuzanne.com $169-$229 incl. breakfast

A RESTAURANT AND BAR FOR LOVERS
CHALET SUZANNE RESTAURANT
There are a number of small dining rooms but the hexagonal one overlooking the peaceful little lake is perhaps the most romantic. Tables are set with a whimsical assortment of china and glassware and even in the daytime, it's a dimly lit and intimate place to dine. Your first night here you are served the Chalet Suzanne six-course dinner, which has been the inn's signature meal for over 50 years. (It includes an appetizer, a famous Chalet Suzanne soup, salad, intermezzo of sherbet, and a choice of entrees and desserts.) The cuisine is rich and some of the selections a little unexpected, but the service is graceful and the meal fills your evening, so just go with the flow, order a nice bottle of wine, enjoy the serene atmosphere, and have a romantic time. Friday and Saturday a pianist adds to the romance. After dinner, take your last glass of wine to a secluded area outside and gaze at the stars.

Breakfast is served from 8 a.m. to 11 a.m. at candlelit tables. Choose eggs benedict, or the scrambled eggs with sausage or bacon and a stack of delicious tiny pancakes (the waitress will tempt you with more little stacks). *Breakfast, lunch, dinner daily. Jackets suggested. $$$$*

CHALET SUZANNE BAR
Have a before-dinner drink in the tiny bar. If no one's around, just pull the bell. The late Carl Henshaw painted the marvelous mural of the marching drummers.

WINE DUNGEON
Duck your head and step down into the tiny Wine Dungeon for the evening mini-wine-tasting. There's barely enough room for two.

ROMANTIC RADIO
Easy: 94.9FM   Jazz: 94.1FM   Classical: 90FM

HELPFUL HINTS: Beware that all meal prices are definitely of the "sticker-shock" variety, so check out the room–meal combination packages.

Directions: I-4, exit 55, south 18 mi. on Rt. 27 to left onto Chalet Suzanne Rd. Go 1-1/2 mi. to right. Or Rt. 60 to Rt. 27, north 4 mi. to right on Chalet Suzanne Rd.). Or fly in to their 2450' grass airstrip.

101

ROMANTIC MONEY SAVERS

The best things in life may not be free, but certainly some of the most romantic things in life do not have to be expensive.

⌘You can have a bottle of Moet & Chandon and some pate and crackers in a hotel dining room for somewhere around $200...or you can also bring your own bottle of Korbel, some vegetarian pate, and some crackers, and have them on your balcony under the stars or in your bathtub for about $20.

⌘After-dinner drinks in a sophisticated lounge or club are certainly romantic and a couple of libations each should run around $36 with tip...or you can pack your own little bottles of cognac or Perrier and enjoy them in bed or walking on a beach for about $6 and no tip.

⌘You can have your inn or resort make you a picnic lunch...or you can find a deli and make your own for half the price.

⌘You can design and enjoy a wonderful day at the spa for a few hundred dollars...or you can give each other a special day at your own private "spa" for next-to-nothing.

⌘You can extract anything you might ever want from your mini-bar at the usual mini-bar prices...or you can bring some of this stuff with you, at supermarket prices.

⌘You can order breakfast from room service...or bring fresh fruit and a bottle of sparkling water for breakfast in bed.

⌘Remember that a single perfect rose waiting to greet your love can be as romantic as all the flowers in the world.

TAKE A TRAIN

If you are coming to Florida from the northeast, try the train. For 20 hours, the landscape of the east coast rolls peacefully by. Before you say "20 hours, no way" stop and think. Twenty hours together in a private compartment with a bed, no phones (turn your cell off), and no interruptions.

In the daylight you see towns go by, including towns you thought no longer existed, with a little main street with a one-floor hardware store and not much else. The train goes by beautiful old houses and through miles and miles of forest and undeveloped land.

Service on this leg of Amtrak isn't exactly flawless, but there is a way to make this a wonderfully romantic adventure. However, don't do this unless both of you like the idea of camping, like to picnic, and you both truly like the idea of being unreachable for 20 hours.

The only compartments conducive to romance are the Deluxe Bedrooms in the Viewliner Sleeping Cars. At night – or whenever you want – the couch pulls out into a bed and a bunk pulls down from the ceiling. Two people can sleep in the bed if you like sleeping entwined (it's a cozy 3' x 6') and one of you can always go to the upper bunk for some serious shut-eye. There's also a little room with a toilet that is also a full shower, with good water pressure and nice hot water.

There is a dining car but don't even THINK of eating the food. Well, breakfast is okay, if you must, but the atmosphere in the dining car is not exactly romantic, and the service couldn't be much worse. So bring your own picnic with you. If you bring your food you can have a nice civilized dinner sitting across from each other in your compartment, watching the world go by. Share a large bottle of water or a fine wine and dine on whatever the two of you like best – get a selection of gourmet salads, some cold chicken, chunks of cheeses, a loaf of French bread, and grapes or apples. Or get thick sandwiches from your local deli. Keep it all in a disposable styrofoam container that you can leave behind. You can eat whatever you didn't finish for the next day's lunch. (Complimentary coffee and packaged pastries or cookies are available.)

The attendant will come and put your bed up or down but not necessarily when you want, so do it yourself. It's easy to do and nice to be in charge, especially on this train. In fact, the only way to do this trip and make it fun and romantic is if you stay in charge.

With all these warnings, why take the train? It's very relaxing to slow down and do almost nothing for 20 hours. It's even more relaxing when you simply can't do anything except sleep, take naps, read, play cards, talk, or think while you watch the scenery drift by. The noise of the wheels against the track and the regular rhythmic motion are soothing and peaceful. But you have to be happy to be out of touch.

Helpful Hints: If you're a water-nut, bring your own (the train water is drinkable but not delicious). Luggage is inaccessible if you check it and not particularly easy to get at during the trip if you stow it in the roomy space above you, so pack a little bag with what you'll need while on board (toiletries, books, glasses). And dress comfortably.
Reservations: Amtrak, 800.872.7245. The round-trip price is similar to two nights of lodging plus airfare for two.

SECTION 3

FLORIDA'S ROMANTIC WEST COAST

SEASIDE
ANNA MARIA ISLAND
SIESTA KEY
KNIGHT'S ISLAND
SANIBEL
NORTH NAPLES

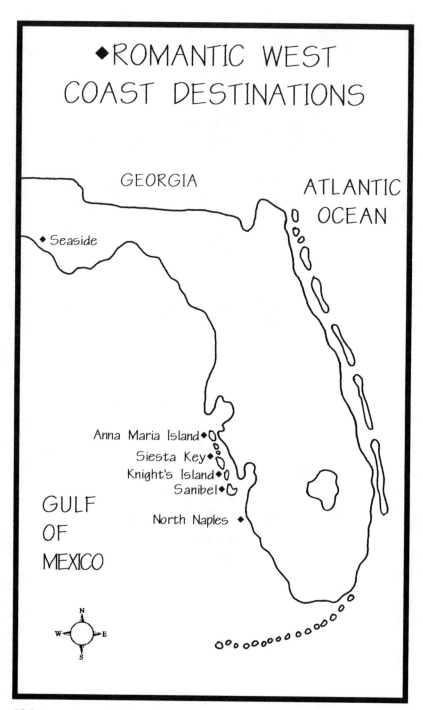

◆ROMANTIC WEST COAST DESTINATIONS

GEORGIA

ATLANTIC OCEAN

◆ Seaside

Anna Maria Island ◆
Siesta Key ◆
Knight's Island ◆
Sanibel ◆

North Naples ◆

GULF OF MEXICO

N
W E
S

CHAPTER 19

A ROMANTIC ESCAPE TO SEASIDE

AN OVERVIEW

Improbably located on an isolated stretch of Florida's panhandle is a remarkable planned community known as Seaside. It's evocative of Nantucket or Martha's Vineyard or even Key West (and if you saw *The Truman Show*, you'll definitely recognize it; the Jim Carey movie was shot here).

This is an astonishing beachside cluster of white picket fences and brick walkways, of little pastel-painted clapboard cottages and wrap-around porches—an 80-acre celebration of creative architectural response to a strict set of design codes.

Almost everything in this casual but sophisticated community is within walking distance. It's very relaxing and people stroll about here. There are antique shops, art galleries, restaurants, boutiques, a bookstore, a wine bar, and a great little market. Walkways lead down to a half-mile stretch of gorgeous beach. For an enchanting romantic escape in Seaside, check yourselves into the charming Josephine's French Country Inn.

LODGING FOR LOVERS
JOSEPHINE'S

This elegant Bed & Breakfast is romantic and relaxing. The two of you can spend hours in your comfortable room in front of the fire or walk to sophisticated restaurants and shops and also to the beach.

A gate in a white picket fence marks the inviting entrance to Josephine's French Country Inn. The building is designed in the manner of a classic Georgian plantation, with imposing two-story columns, stately chimneys at each end, and wide verandas off both floors.

Each unit is different but all are nicely decorated with a mix of antique and reproduction furniture. Rooms have a little kitchen alcove with a sink, a microwave, and a small refrigerator, and most have working fireplaces. The spacious suites are next to the main building and have a living room, a dining area, a separate bedroom, a full kitchen, and a working fireplace. Two of the suites also have whirlpool tubs. The most romantic choices are the two suites with views of the Gulf. A full gourmet breakfast in included in the rate.

This is a place to come to relax. You can walk everywhere. Spend your days at the gorgeous beach where the sand is dazzling white and the Gulf is a sheer Caribbean aquamarine. Or wander about the small town. There are often scheduled events held in the amphitheater in the village green. Despite the sophistication of Seaside, dress is casual here and the two of you can pack light.

Smoking outside only. No children. Check-out 11 a.m. 9 units (7 with fireplaces). Innkeepers: Bruce and Judy Albert. 101 Seaside Ave. (mail address: P.O. Box 4767), Seaside, 32459. Res: 800.848.1840. Tel: 850.231.1940. Fax: 850.231.2446. Web:www.josephinesinn.com $200-$250

> About two-thirds of the houses in the Seaside community are available for rent, including some honeymoon cottages that are right on the beach. Contact **Seaside Cottage Rental Agency** *(800.277.8696, www.seasidefl.com)* if you are interested.

A RESTAURANT FOR LOVERS
SANDOR'S
A five-minute drive from the inn is this tiny and delightful restaurant specializing in European cuisine exquisitely prepared by the remarkable Chef Sandor. There are only eight tables and the atmosphere is decidedly romantic. The menu changes but choices might include rack of lamb with lentils, caramelized cauliflower, and Moroccan-spice sauce; lobster ravioli with wild mushrooms; or local grouper with truffle butter and a port and sherry reduction sauce. *Reservations a must. Dinner nightly. CR395, Seagrove Beach, 850.231.2858 $$$*

ROMANTIC THINGS TO DO HERE
Rent a kayak from Cabana Man (*George's Gorge, 850.231.5046*).

Have a custom-blend of bath oils created just for the two of you. Talk to the staff at Patchouli's (*Four Corners, 850.231.1447*).

Create a picnic for the beach from the gourmet selections at the marvelous Modica Market (*Central Sq., 850.231.1214*).

Stop in for an evening of jazz and blues at Bud & Alley's popular rooftop bar (*Cinderella Cir., 850.231.5900*).

Have a photograph taken of the two of you embracing on the beach in the glorious Florida sunset. Call Seashore Portraits (*850.231.5755*).

Share a glass of wine and some cheese at Fermentations Wine Bar (*25 Central Sq., 850.231.0167*). Choose from over 40 wines by the glass. Go to a tasting every Wednesday, Friday, and Saturday at 4:30 p.m.

Try an Italian ice at Cafe Spiaggia (*2236 Hwy. 38, 850.231.1297*).

ROMANTIC RADIO
Easy: 95FM Country: 102FM Oldies: 1450AM

HELPFUL HINTS: This is a truly casual destination, even at Sandor's.

Directions: I-10, Exit 85. Go south on Rt. 331 to Rt. 98. Turn left (east) on Rt. 98. Take first right (south) onto CR283, then first left onto Rt. 30A to Seaside.

A FEW TIME-TESTED ROMANTIC SURPRISES

Mail your lover a love letter or a love poem that will arrive before you do and be waiting when you check in.

Arrange for a bouquet of balloons, or a box of candy, or a favorite bottle of wine to be waiting in the room when you open the door.

Send ahead a photo album of your own pictures and some other personal stuff to reminisce and laugh about. Ask that it be set out on a table in your room just before you arrive.

Have a gift-wrapped present delivered to your lover in your room, or to the pool, or to your table at dinner.

If there is live music wherever the two of you are headed, secretly arrange "your song" to be played sometime during your evening.

Ask to have your bed made up with satin sheets.

Arrange for a bouquet of flowers to be hidden in the shower. Or a ring to be under the pillow.

Make plans for a special room service presentation that is delivered unexpectedly.

CHAPTER 20

A ROMANTIC ESCAPE TO ANNA MARIA ISLAND

AN OVERVIEW

Remarkably peaceful Anna Maria Island lies just northwest of Sarasota on the Gulf of Mexico and boasts a spectacular beach. It's seven miles long, extremely wide, and rimmed with tall and graceful Australian pines, some as high as 60 feet.

When you want to escape to one of the most enchanting getaways in Florida, just head to Anna Maria Island and the exquisitely romantic Harrington House, which is much more than a Bed & Breakfast. It's tucked between sea grapes right smack on the beach and, remarkably, within walking distance of one of the state's very finest restaurants.

This is a place to come when the two of you want to spend days in bare feet, napping under a tree with a book in your lap, waking to take a dip in the pool and then another in the Gulf. One, some, or even every evening, you can put on something a little fancy, and walk on the beach, shoes in hand, to the intimate and immensely enjoyable Beach Bistro for an exceptionally elegant and romantic dinner.

LODGING FOR LOVERS
HARRINGTON HOUSE

At this delightful beachfront Bed & Breakfast complex, your days are measured in large, romantic, relaxing chunks: late sleeps, long naps, lingering beach walks, leisurely dining, and even nightcaps by the fire.

The entrance here is outstanding. A narrow path leads through tall trees and fragrant tropical flowers to a simple arched doorway. As you pass under the arch and into a little outdoor courtyard the world behind slips away and you feel as if you've actually crossed a magic threshold.

Rooms are in five buildings and all have a balcony or patio, a TV/VCR, and a little fridge (a few have kitchens). If you want to be in a traditional Bed & Breakfast, choose the three-story main house, a frame building dating from 1925. Seven rooms are individually decorated with a mixture of furnishings, nicely wallpapered or painted, and some have beds facing directly out to the Gulf so the two of you can actually lie in bed and take in the view. Next door is the tiny Honeymoon Cottage with a pink, heart-shaped jetted tub. Also next door are the Spangler Beach House, with four rooms, and the Dodt House, with three apartments. A five-minute walk up the beach is the newer Huth Beach House, with four romantic rooms, two with jetted tubs, and all with gas fireplaces. From Huth Beach House, breakfast is a walk away, but the outstanding Beach Bistro is right next door and you can step over for dinner or have it served, course by course, on your private terrace!

In the cozy living room of the main house, comfortable couches are arranged around a wood-burning fireplace. Floor-to-ceiling shelves hold books and video tapes. There's a menu for every restaurant within about 20 miles, popcorn in the early evening and, always, a plate of just-baked chocolate chip cookies. There are tables for two in the charming breakfast rooms. Outside is a good-size pool and beyond that the seven-mile beach.

Pool, bikes, kayaks. Smoking outside only. No children under 13. Check-out 11 a.m. 19 units. Innkeepers: Davis family. 5626 Gulf Dr., Holmes Beach, Anna Maria Island, 34217. Res: 888.828.5566. Tel: 941.778.5444. Fax: 941.778.0527. Web: www.harringtonhouse.com $139-$329

RESTAURANTS FOR LOVERS
BEACH BISTRO
One of the many great things about staying at the Harrington House is that, depending on where your room is, you are either a short walk (or a one-minute drive) or right next to Sean Murphy's exceptionally romantic, award-winning restaurant, the Beach Bistro, one of Florida's best. It's small and elegant and built right on the beach with wall-to-wall windows that show off the Gulf and the sunset, but the view is incidental. You come for the outstanding quality and preparation of the cuisine, the unobtrusively fine service, and the hushed, dark, and intimate atmosphere. The menu is interesting and creative, the fish outstandingly fresh, and the beef the best you can buy. Try the tournedos of tenderloin with a peppery cognac demi-glace, or the roast duck with berry sauce, or the "Kicker" grilled jumbo shrimp. From the signature starter, the very unclassic lobsterscargots, to the very classic Bananas Foster, you can't go wrong here. *Reservations necessary. Dinner nightly. 6600 Gulf Dr., 941.778.6444 $$-$$$*

ISLAND'S END
Luckily for everyone, Beach Bistro owner Sean Murphy decided to open a second restaurant on Anna Maria Island. This one's a bit more casual (although it still has tablecloths) and quite a bit larger, with a number of rooms and a large bar. It's also a bit more whimsical, from the bright turquoise exterior trim to the artsy photographs to the laid-back, highly original cuisine. Try the Beastro burger with smoked cheddar, the "Better than any Frenchman's" onion soup, Aunt Renie's Chicken Pot Pie, or the superb pizzas. Hungrier diners can choose from such specialities as a Gulf Coast bouillabaisse, Key West flash-grilled shrimp, free-range rotisseried chicken, or the pasta of the day. Bananas Foster, New Orleans bread pudding, and Key Lime Pie are just some of the tempting desserts. *Dinner nightly. 10101 Gulf Dr., 941.779.2444 $$*

ROMANTIC THINGS TO DO HERE
Bike over to Mama Lo's By the Sea *(101 S. Bay Blvd., 941.779.1288)* for a double-scoop ice cream cone or a chocolate sundae. Choose from a zillion flavors of ice cream. Or have an espresso, or a simple lunch of a PB&J, a BLT, or a hot dog.

113

Look for shooting stars and constellations. Pull beach chairs down near the water's edge and gaze up at the stunning night sky scenery. Don't forget to make a wish when you see a shooting star (and don't forget to pull your chair back where you found it).

Bike over to the end of one of the fishing piers on the east side of the island for an amazing faraway view of the Skyway Bridge and Tampa.

Rent a pontoon boat and explore the bay. Call Cortez Watercraft Rentals *(941.792.5263)* and spend the morning out on the water. Half- day rentals are $139, full days are $179, both plus fuel and tax.

Pick out a sexy camisole or some slinky pants at the Beach Style Boutique *(10010 Gulf Dr., 941.778.4323)* or buy candles, housewares, or an upscale T-shirt.

For a sophisticated lunch and a potpourri of shops, head down to classy St. Armand's Circle. You'll find art galleries, resortwear for men and women, beach shops and more, plus a wide variety of restaurants, many with outdoor seating. It's an easy 20-minute drive.

Dine in the casually romantic Sign of the Mermaid *(9707 Gulf Dr., 941.778.9399)*, cozily set in a tiny old Florida house.

Browse around the unusual shops in Bay View Plaza *(101 S. Bay Blvd.)*, on the east side of the island across from the fishing pier.

Thrill yourselves with a parasail ride. Cortez Parasail *(Cortez Rd., 941.795.2700)* will take you up for a memorable "sail!" You can go up together at the same time for about $100.

ROMANTIC RADIO
Easy: 88.1FM   Jazz: 94.1FM   Classical: 90FM

HELPFUL HINTS: Avoid driving to or from St. Armand's Circle on-season during rush hour or you could be stuck in traffic for hours.

Directions: I-75, exit 220/220B. Go west 11 mi. on Rt. 64 to Rt. 789 (Gulf Dr.) and turn right (north). Be sure to stay on Gulf Dr. (it twists here and there).

SHARING

Whether the two of you are sharing your lives together or just a few footprints in the sand, try sharing some of the ideas below on your next romantic escape.

Share your meals. Order foods you both want to taste or try, and share your choices. It can be breakfast in bed, a picnic lunch, or a special dinner. Or order meals made tableside for two, like a classic Caesar salad, or chateaubriand, or tasty cherries jubilee.

Share a book. Take turns reading aloud to one another from a book you'll both enjoy together, or get two copies of the same book and read them together, separately.

Share "back-to-back" massages. Give each other a half-hour massage after a tough day of relaxing and before your evening bath or shower together.

Share a sensuous shampoo session. Or dry each other's hair. If one partner is hirsutely challenged, then a scalp massage is nice.

Share a carafe of wine. Or a bottle of mineral water. Or a pitcher of juice. Pour for each other.

Share some silence together. During a long walk on the beach, or while on a bench in the park, a canoe on a lake, or just silently holding each other in bed.

Share paying or signing for everything. It doesn't matter whose money actually is paying. Share the joy of the act of "buying" things for each other.

THE MOST ROMANTIC FROM A TO Z

Afterhours Dancing: Polo Lounge
Brunch: Registry
Cuban Coffee: Spanish River Grill
Dinner: Beach Bistro
Entrance: Harrington House and Song of the Sea
Fireplaces: Fairbanks House and Governors Inn
Gallery: Morse Museum
Hot Tubs: Turtle Beach Resort
Italian Restaurant: Renato's
Jazz: Heidelberg
Kayaking: Registry
Library: Chesterfield
Moonlit Walk: Palm Island Resort
Nightclub: Club Zanzibar
Open Air Lunch: Toni and Joe's
Piano During Dinner: Portofino
Quiet Beach: Anna Maria Island
Room Service Menu: Chesterfield
Sexiest Bedroom: Riverside Hotel
Two-Person Bar: Chalet Suzanne
Understated Elegance: Chesterfield
Views: Ritz-Carlton Amelia Island
Wine List: Beach Bistro
X-rated Ceiling: Leopard Lounge
Yellowfin Tuna: Spanish River Grill
Ziti: Tra Vini

CHAPTER 21

A ROMANTIC ESCAPE TO SIESTA KEY

AN OVERVIEW

Siesta Key is a long, slender barrier island just east of Sarasota and has good shelling beaches facing the Gulf of Mexico. It's primarily a residential island and the scenery along the main road switches back and forth from gated private driveways with manicured hedges and hidden mansions to the occasional mid-rise condo set amidst an expanse of carefully-tended lawn.

Tucked along the edge of the peaceful Intracoastal Waterway on the very narrow and residential (and non-trafficky) south end of the island is tiny and romantic Turtle Beach Resort, a cluster of funky cottages, each with a complete kitchen and its own private outdoor hot tub. There are hammocks slung here and there in the tropical greenery. There's a pool overlooking the waterway and a little dock with canoes and rowboats. The Gulf and a great beach are a three-minute walk away. Right next door is one of Sarasota's most romantic restaurants.

What more could you ask for?

LODGING FOR LOVERS
TURTLE BEACH RESORT

This romantic cluster of cottages, each with a private outdoor hot tub, is a one-of-a-kind spot. It's casual and funky and feels a bit like Key West or the Caribbean.

This delightful escape is right on the water, on an offshoot of the Intracoastal Waterway. It looks impossibly small when you drive up to it, and indeed, cottages are in a compact cluster, but they are extremely private inside. Studios and one- and two-bedroom units have VCRs and full kitchens, and each also has its own very private hot tub.

Things are laid-back here. Cottages are casually decorated and each has a loosely-followed theme. The Southwestern Cottage features a Mexican tile shower. Country French has a four-poster bed. The Country Cottage is sort of "Pier 1" country. Most have some sort of water view and several cottages are right on the water.

The grounds are dense with tropical greenery. There's a heated pool overlooking the Intracoastal Waterway, hammocks big enough for two, and several little docks. The water views are superbly peaceful. It's incredibly easy to be here. You have a full kitchen, but if you don't want to cook, just walk next door to Ophelia's on the Bay. It's one of the best restaurants in the Sarasota area and they'll even deliver a romantic dinner right to your cottage! You can walk to the most unpopulated beach on Siesta Key in three minutes and swim or sit in the sun or go shelling. You can also take a rowboat or canoe or paddleboat to a very private strip of sand reachable only by boat.

It is the innkeepers here who really make a difference and if you want something special, just ask. Beware that children are welcome and could be heard playing outside in such a compact place.

Pool, dock, canoes, rowboats, kayak, paddleboat, fishing poles, bikes. Maid service additional. Check-out by 11 a.m. 10 cottages. Innkeepers: Gail and Dave Rubinfeld. 9049 Midnight Pass Rd., Siesta Key, 34242. Tel: 941.349.4554. Fax: 941.918.0203. Web: www.turtlebeachresort.com $190-$385

RESTAURANTS FOR LOVERS
OPHELIA'S ON THE BAY
This romantic and elegant gem is right on the water, right next door to the Turtle Beach Resort. Reserve a table along the wall of windows in one of the two romantically-lit dining rooms or on the outside deck and gaze at the peaceful, placid waterway. If you are there at twilight, watch the colors of the water change and look for dolphins swimming along. Start with the eggplant crepes, the chicken and asparagus soup, or the semolina-coated crab cake. For entrees, the filet mignon with porcini demi-glace, the black grouper, or the pork tenderloin are excellent choices. *Dinner nightly. 9105 Midnight Pass Rd., 941.349.2212 $$-$$$*

SUMMERHOUSE
For a romantic setting, this has to be one of the best anywhere. The dining room walls are all solid glass, floor-to-ceiling, invisible windows that define the edges of a forest. Everywhere you look there are trees and more trees, deftly lit at night. A series of angles means that most tables are windowside and diners are treated to a stunning, awesome view of a tropical mix of trees, plants, and stately trunks that come right up to the glass. It's a true pleasure, in an airy, intimate, romantic setting like this, to find out that the cuisine here is excellent, too. Escargot in pastry or seared ahi tuna are tasty starters. Then try grouper piccata, grilled mahi mahi, shrimp with spaghettini, or the outstanding tournedos Rossini, with foie gras and port wine sauce. *Dinner nightly. 6101 Midnight Pass Rd., 941.349.1100 $$-$$$*

BELLA ROMA
Improbably placed on the upstairs level of a small strip mall, this cozy and delightful Italian restaurant is an intimate spot to share an evening meal. The booths along the window are perhaps the most romantic. Count on classically-prepared Italian cuisine: eggplant rollatine, fried mozzarella, or roasted red peppers for tasty appetizers; homemade stracciatella and minestrone soups; and for the main course, traditional lasagna, ravioli stuffed with spinach and ricotta, veal marsala, veal saltimbocca, grilled salmon with gorgonzola sauce, or the risotta with porcini mushrooms prepared for two. *Dinner nightly. 5239 Ocean Blvd., 941.349.0995 $$*

ROMANTIC THINGS TO DO HERE

Head out to the little dock and watch the show. Look for dolphins. They often travel in pairs. Watch the pelicans dive-bomb for dinner. Keep an eye out for jumping schools of fish.

Canoe or row to the secluded beach that's just five minutes away.

Drive up to tiny Siesta Village and the little cluster of shops and restaurants. Get a double-scoop ice cream cone, or a bathing suit, or even have lunch.

Walk over to the beach just before sunset time and see if you can catch the green flash.

Have a private massage for two outside by your hot tub.

Walk through the very aromatic Organic Herb Garden at the Summerhouse (*6101 Midnight Pass Rd., 941.349.1100*).

Rent a little boat and drift for hours. The waterway here has lots of places to explore and you can spend hours putt-putting around. You can even fish for your dinner. Call Mr. C. B.'s (*1249 Stickney Point Rd., 941.349.4400*) and go out on a little 17' motorboat.

When you want a picnic for a boat trip or the beach, head up the road to delightful Anna's Delicatessen (*6535 Midnight Pass Rd., 941.349.4888*). Sandwiches are really BIG here, but you can get them by the half if you want.

ROMANTIC RADIO
Easy: 88.1FM   Jazz: 94.1FM   Classical: 90FM

HELPFUL HINTS: Bear in mind that the town is a very popular winter destination. Turtle Beach Resort happens to be in the quietest section of Siesta Key. Be prepared for traffic if you drive north on the island, and be prepared for lots of traffic if you head to the mainland.

Directions: I-75, exit 205. Go west 5 mi. over Stickney Point Bridge to left onto Midnight Pass Rd. Go south 3 mi.

ROMANTIC MOVIES

If there's a VCR at your romantic escape, bring along some of your favorite tapes. Watching a video together during breakfast, or at midnight, or after a strenuous assortment of activities can be a wonderful, relaxing treat.

And since being in love means laughing and loving and hoping and crying together, the movie choices can be vast. Following is an eclectic gathering of suggestions. Bring some of these or favorites of your own along.

The Bridges of Madison County
Breakfast at Tiffany's
Gone With the Wind
Ghost
Shadowlands
Love Story
Casablanca
Sleepless in Seattle
A Robin Williams tape
You've Got Mail
A Comic Relief tape
One of Peter Seller's Pink Panther series
Message in a Bottle
A Stephen Wright tape
Stir Crazy
A Massage for Lovers tape
My Big Fat Greek Wedding
An adult selection
Singin' in the Rain
The French Lieutenant's Woman
The Brothers McMullen

MORE ROMANTIC IDEAS

☐Spell "I love you" for your love in flower petals.

☐Try stone crab if you are here during the season (October 15 to May 15). It's delicious hot or cold.

☐Buy something. Big, small, inexpensive, or not. Just buy a "memory" of this escape.

☐Fill the tub up with bubbles and settle in. Two people can fit in even the standard-size tubs at the resorts in this book.

☐Have some oysters (cooked, not raw) or some green M&Ms. Four oysters are supposed to be the minimum for those remarkable romantic results. No one has yet studied how many green M&Ms it takes.

☐Plan your vacation around the full moon.

☐Plan a trip for your partner but don't say where you are going. Just write a list of what to bring. Or do all the packing yourself.

☐Look for glittering phosphorous at night in the water or even in the seaweed on the beach. Just step on the seaweed and you can see it light up.

☐Give a "trip" gift certificate to your love for a birthday or anniversary. Most lodgings in this book offer them. Or you can create your own.

CHAPTER 22

A ROMANTIC ESCAPE TO KNIGHT'S ISLAND

AN OVERVIEW

Knight's Island lies off of Florida's southwest coast just west of tiny Cape Haze and north of Fort Myers. It's the setting for very remote Palm Island Resort. When the two of you want to get away from everything, even cars, head to this isolated escape with its two miles of pristine beach and no bridge to the mainland. Cars aren't allowed past the parking lot. You catch a car ferry over and then park for good.

There's not much action here, and what little there is, is of the natural kind. This is a place of laid-back romance, of lazy days and peaceful starlit nights. There's one restaurant and bar but units include full kitchens and if you are coming for more than a weekend, you will want to bring groceries. Families come here because it's a safe place to let kids roam, so there will be children. But generally you can find your own romantic space, inside or out. The resort is incredibly relaxing, but skip it if your idea of romance includes lots of pampering or fancy restaurant dinners. You're pretty much on your own here and the romantic dinners you have will be the ones you cook yourselves.

LODGING FOR LOVERS
PALM ISLAND RESORT

You won't be pampered at this 200-acre island retreat that looks out at the Gulf of Mexico, but for two people who want to be really alone together and relax, it's a great romantic spot. It's hard to imagine how laid-back this place is until you actually get here and experience it. You can truly spend days here without putting on shoes.

Accommodations are in three-story, pale gray frame buildings with Old Florida-style tin roofs. The one-bedroom apartments facing the water (called Gulf Front Beach Villas) are perfect for a romantic escape. The layout makes great use of 800 square feet and you can live here comfortably. The living-dining area opens onto a balcony perfect for coffee or a candlelit dinner. The kitchen is fully equipped.

You won't find a lot of hangers in the closets here because no one who comes here needs many clothes. In the summer months you could easily get by with a bathing suit or two, a cover-up, something with long sleeves for breezy nights or protection from the sun, and a bathrobe for breakfast on the balcony. So pack light. Use the extra luggage space for books, your favorite videos, or if you are into gourmet cooking, unusual culinary items for your romantic dinners.

Maid service is not included but is available daily or twice weekly for a charge. There's a washer/dryer in the unit and extra towels and it's actually quite relaxing to never have someone knock on your door.

Catch the car ferry at the marina on the mainland (check-in is on the island). The ferry makes the run back and forth from 7 a.m. until 10 p.m. (11 p.m. on weekends). A "people-only" boat also operates from noon until evening, for those who want to dine at Leverocks Restaurant at the marina or for those boaters who want to come to the Rum Bay Restaurant for dinner.

Restaurant, bar, 5 pools, 11 tennis courts and pro shop, horseshoes, store. Check-out 11 a.m. 160 apartments with full kitchens. 7092 Placida Rd., Cape Haze, 33946. Res: 800.824.5412. Tel: 941.697.4800. Fax: 941.697.0696. Web: www.palmisland.com $205-$360

RUM BAY RESTAURANT AND BAR

This is the only restaurant on the island and it's not open for breakfast. Despite the fact that it can be busy and sometimes filled with children, the atmosphere is still quite pleasant. The food is simple but good and the menu is nicely varied—baby back ribs, grilled local grouper or shrimp, burgers, pizzas, vegetarian dishes, salads, pastas. The bar features happy hour "island drinks." *Daily 11:30 a.m.-9:30p.m. $-$$*

ROMANTIC THINGS TO DO HERE

Rent a little power boat and drift through the mangroves. You can also rent canoes, snorkel equipment, kayaks, windsurfers, and bikes.

Sign up for a turtle walk and learn how they are protected here.

Go fishing. Even if you never have. Bait and fishing tackle can be rented and it's pretty easy to catch a fish in these waters.

Watch for falling stars. Pull a beach chair down to the water's edge, snuggle together and just look up at the glorious night sky.

Look for the green flash at sunset from your balcony.

If you get island fever, take a cruise to see the sunset, or to Useppa Island for the day, or go to Leverock's on the mainland for dinner.

ROMANTIC RADIO
Easy: 104.9FM

HELPFUL HINTS: Bring bathrobes (you'll be in them more than anything else), prescription meds, shampoo or anything you are fussy about (the little convenience store has the basics but not necessarily your brand), sturdy shoes for walking the rockier parts of the shoreline, candles for romantic dinners, and your favorite wines and champagnes. You can rent VCRs and tapes, but bring your favorites. The on-island store has mostly frozen and canned goods and your best bet is to stop at a supermarket on the way. Do get some special treats. This is a great place to prepare some romantic meals together.

Directions: I-75, exit 191. Right on River Rd. Cross US 41. Continue 7 mi. to traffic light at Pine St. Turn left and go 7 mi. to large ferry sign on right.

I will always love you

(following is an anniversary note — written from the heart)

I will always love you

I will never leave you

I will be by your side and stay by your side
as long as we shall live (and beyond)

You are the love of my life
I did not know love like this existed
but I had always hoped

I found true love when I found you

I also found love with you was
even better than I had ever imagined

You are the love of my life, my love

I love you every moment
from the night when you are sleeping by my side
to the morning when you wake up and smile at me
to the evening again when you touch me
or hold me by your side

I miss you when we are apart and
love the things we do together
whether we are playing or working or just being

I love you

CHAPTER 23

A ROMANTIC ESCAPE TO SANIBEL ISLAND

AN OVERVIEW

Sanibel is a barrier island off the coast of Fort Myers in southwest Florida. It's connected to the mainland by a three-mile-long causeway. Both sides of the island are spectacular. Shell-filled beaches face out to the Gulf of Mexico. Across the island are wetlands and marshes and beautiful San Carlos Bay which is sprinkled with hundreds of tiny green puffs of uninhabited islets.

Sanibel Island is far enough south to be almost always warm and is a popular winter destination. There are many resorts and motels here and the one main road that runs the length of the island can be incredibly trafficky in the winter months. For a romantic escape on Sanibel, nothing beats the Song of the Sea. Off the traveled path, it's a small, secluded hideaway set back from the beach among palm trees and Australian pines. Comfortable condo-like units have full kitchens but the rest of the property is more like an inn, from the cozy common living room where a scrumptious continental breakfast is served, to the caring management, to room service from the excellent restaurant that is right next door.

LODGING FOR LOVERS
SONG OF THE SEA

At this charming and secluded beachfront prize, you can really relax. You can live in your bathing suit and cook in your room, walk to an excellent restaurant (which will also deliver), spend your days looking for shells or biking, or order a pizza in and watch a movie on the VCR.

From the moment you arrive here, you know this place is special. The entrance is terrific. You check in at a little desk in a warm, welcoming living room and then you drive through an archway and you know you've escaped to a peaceful world.

Rooms are in appealing two-story pink stucco buildings. They aren't romantically decorated but they are exceptionally comfortable and easy to relax in. If you want some space and an unbeatable view, go for the beachfront one-bedroom suites. There's a dark and cozy bedroom that you can sleep in all day. A full kitchen runs along the hallway to the dining and living area. Sliding glass doors lead to a large, private balcony. The view is picture-perfect: green grass, sand dunes, striped beach umbrellas in a row, the turquoise Gulf beyond.

The grounds are grassy and there's an outdoor grill (if you feel like cooking out) and a nice-size pool. The beach is full of shells and you can clean off your finds of the day in the little "shelling" hut.

Everything is easy here. For breakfast, delicious rolls, breads, fruits, and pastries are laid out. Toss a coin and see which one of you brings it back on the thoughtfully provided trays. For dinner, the two of you can walk next door to Portofino, an excellent Italian restaurant. Or dial 316 and they'll deliver right to your room.

It's incredibly peaceful and quiet here and very removed from the hustle and bustle of much of Sanibel.

Pool, whirlpool, grill, bicycles, shuffleboard. Check-out 11 a.m. 30 units. General Manager: Linda Logan. 863 East Gulf Dr., Sanibel Island, 33957. Res: 800.231.1045. Tel: 239.472.2220. Fax: 239.472.8569. Web: www.songofthesea.com $185-$445

RESTAURANTS FOR LOVERS
PORTOFINO
Next door to the Song of the Sea is this intimate and romantic northern Italian restaurant. A pianist plays gentle background music Thursday through Sunday. Low walls and groupings of plants create numerous discrete dining areas. Do listen to the evening specials. If you want anything not on the menu, just ask. Sharing the antipasto for two is a perfect way to begin the meal together here. The minestrone or any of the salads are also good choices. For an entree, try the veal saltimbocca, or veal marsala, or any of the pasta dishes. The rich bolognese sauce comes with fettucini but it's also excellent over spaghetti. If you want them to deliver to your room, just call. *Dinner nightly. 937 East Gulf Dr., 239.472.0494 $$*

WINDOWS ON THE WATER
This restaurant is in a resort and you have to walk through a sometimes hectic reception area to get here, but once you step inside you'll find a quiet, intimate atmosphere. Tables are on two levels and diners have a terrific view of the Gulf through floor-to-ceiling windows. Dine on surf and turf, local grouper, seafood pad Thai, or their signature dish, tender "Duck Noopie." *Lunch, dinner daily. Sundial Beach Resort, 1451 Middle Gulf Dr., 239.395.6014 $$*

THISTLE LODGE
This appealing restaurant overlooks the Gulf of Mexico and is designed to resemble a Victorian-style house, but with floor-to-ceiling windows that show off the view. Tables are in several small rooms and arranged so that most have great water views. Entrees include Florida lobster thermador, a spicy seafood paella, Jamaican jerk pork, and grilled N.Y. strip with a rum-barbeque sauce. *Lunch, dinner daily. Casa Ybel Resort, 2255 West Gulf Dr., 239.472.9200 $$*

ROMANTIC THINGS TO DO HERE
Get married or renew your vows barefoot on the beach at sunset or even romantically drifting along in a boat. Call Patricia Slater at Weddings By the Sea (*239.472.8712*). Sometimes she only needs a few hours advance notice, so you can almost "get married again" on the spur of the moment!

129

Go to a spa together. Try a relaxing aromatherapy massage, or a honeysuckle scrub, or a warm herbal wrap, or splurge and get a his-and-hers Royal Spoil—a full day of gentle pampering, or create your very own package. Call Day Spa of Sanibel (*2075 Periwinkle Way at Periwinkle Pl., 239.395.2220*) for a complete list of services.

Stop in the 32 little shops at Periwinkle Place. The Brown Bag (*239.472.1171*) carries casual clothes for men. The Beach House (*239.472.2676*) has an enormous selection of swimsuits, including Gottex and Elizabeth Stewart. At Island Style (*239.472.4343*) you'll find one-of-a-kind pieces of jewelry, pottery, and sculpture.

Buy each other a surprise gift. You'll find pendants, bracelets, necklaces, and earrings fashioned into shells and exquisitely delicate dolphins at Sanibel Goldsmith (*2055 Periwinkle Way, 239.472.8677*).

For an incredibly romantic moonlit evening on the water, call Wildside Adventures (*15041 Captiva Dr. at McCarthy's Marina, 239.395.2925*). They'll lead just the two of you (in your own two-person kayak) out to the middle of calm Pine Island Sound on a starlit or moonlit night. You can also rent a two-person kayak or a canoe and paddle around by yourselves during the day.

Check out the J.N. "Ding" Darling National Wildlife Preserve. It covers half of the island and is home to numerous birds, turtles, marsh hares, bobcats, and alligators. Bike or drive the five-mile Wildlife Drive, or hike the trails, or go canoeing. If you want to spot great birds, come just after dawn or just before dusk.

ROMANTIC RADIO
Easy: 104.1FM   Country: 92.9FM Oldies: 100FM

HELPFUL HINTS: Song of the Sea is in a secluded, untrafficky section of Sanibel. Bear in mind that there are few main roads on the island and, in winter, expect to encounter heavy traffic if you plan to venture onto the main thoroughfare of Sanibel or want to head up to Captiva or over to the mainland.

Directions: I-75, exit 131. Take Daniels Rd. West. Cross US41. Continue across Sanibel Cswy. Continue straight through 4-way stop at Periwinkle Way. Go 1/4 mi. and turn left at next stop sign to 1st driveway on right.

130

Dawdle, Cuddle, and Snuggle

And a few other things you should definitely do
while on your next romantic escape

Invent a word to describe the two of you as a couple.

Be thankful that you found each other.

Be a little bit naughty.

Practice opening your hearts and listening
to what they are saying.

Put a message in a bottle and toss it in the ocean.

Make plans together for future escapes.

Go to bed especially early or stay up especially late.

Forget the rules.

Read the Sunday paper in bed together. Share it.

Make two promises to each other...and keep them.

Be thankful together...for everything you have.

Discuss your accomplishments...each of your many
separate accomplishments and your
accomplishments together.

Make a smile the first thing you put on
every morning.

WHO'S IN CHARGE HERE, ANYWAY?

You two are. You're going on a special romantic retreat and you're paying for it. You're in charge. From choosing your special journey to returning home to a special evening, the two of you are in control.

The first way to take control is be sure you choose the "escape" that you really want. They're all great in their own way. Make sure their way matches yours.

If you have any questions, call the property. These properties are here partially because they do special things for people in love. They'll answer any questions and help you with choices.

If a property has a special "romance package" don't be afraid to ask them to "personalize" it for the two of you. If they offer a welcome bottle of champagne and you'd rather have a chardonnay or orange juice, ask!

The properties in this book respond well to requests. So do many of the restaurants. That's one of the reasons they were included here.

For example, if you want to sleep in all day, put out a "do not disturb" sign and tell the desk/innkeeper you want absolutely no calls except emergencies. If you want something not on the menu, ask. If you want softer or more pillows, ask. From flowers to flute music, from balloons to bagels, whatever you want to have or have happen, just ask.

CHAPTER 24

A ROMANTIC ESCAPE TO NORTH NAPLES

AN OVERVIEW

A small section of southwest Florida is not bordered by barrier islands and the western edge of the mainland is one long stunning stretch of beach that looks right out to the Gulf of Mexico. At the south end of this strip is the affluent and sophisticated town of Naples. In the last few years there has been tremendous development just to the north of downtown, and what was once extremely rural is now an exclusive neighborhood known as North Naples, with its own set of fine restaurants and fancy shops.

North Naples has many lodging choices, but for a truly romantic escape, nothing beats the Registry Resort. When the two of you want to stay in a classy, full-service hotel that you won't want to leave— with a great restaurant, an elegant bar, a disco, one of the best Sunday brunches anywhere, a nature preserve, a beach on the Gulf of Mexico, and a spa for massages and herbal wraps— but you also want the choice of many sophisticated restaurants and even the symphony practically out your front door, this is the place to come.

LODGING FOR LOVERS
REGISTRY RESORT

It's the resort itself and the experience of being here that makes it so romantic. The service is superb and if it rained for your entire stay you could still have a wonderfully romantic time.

The Registry is an 18-story high-rise that looks out over the mangroves of Clam Pass Sanctuary and beyond to the Gulf of Mexico. Guest rooms are painted in deep shades of pink or green and heavy draperies keep out the light when you want to sleep. This is a room you can stay in all day, sending down for meals, curled up in thick terry Registry bathrobes, watching movies and snoozing. From your balcony you can scan the twinkling night sky or watch the sun slip into the Gulf.

The resort is truly self-contained. In the lobby is an elegant bar (afternoon tea is served here), a great gift shop, the award-winning Lafite restaurant, and Cafe Chablis and its fabulous Sunday brunch. On a boardwalk just outside the lobby is an ice cream and patisserie shop, several terrific little boutiques, an art gallery, and the Brass Pelican for steak and seafood. Next door is the Club Zanzibar disco.

There's a terrific spa with exercise equipment that faces the view. Come here together for a his-and-hers algae full body mask, or get yourselves wrapped in sea mud, or have therapeutic massages together in the privacy of your room.

When the two of you feel like enjoying the outdoor possibilities, there's plenty to do without leaving the resort. Go for a swim or sit by the pool. Take a tram ride or walk along the half-mile boardwalk to the beach. Learn to sail a Hobie Cat or rent a canoe or a kayak and explore the quiet waters of Clam Pass Sanctuary. Take a tennis lesson for two or get a bicycle for two (rent them at the Towel Stand) and pedal around the quiet residential streets of Pelican Bay.

4 restaurants, beach grill, 3 bars, 24-hour room service, 5 pools, spa, 15 tennis courts and pro shop, golf (6 mi. away). Many non-smoking floors. Check-out noon. 474 rooms. 475 Seagate Dr., Naples, 33940. Res: 800.247.9810. Tel: 239.597.3232. Fax: 239.597.3147. Web: www.registryhotel.com $165-$395

A RESTAURANT FOR LOVERS
LAFITE
When you are in the mood for an elegant and romantic dinner, step into the celebrated Lafite, with walls of rich, dark wood and dim light softly glowing from the candles on the tables and the ceiling chandeliers. There are several intimate dining rooms and the atmosphere is quiet and formal. The innovative, globally-inspired menu changes yearly but includes such creations as pine nut-crusted goat cheese, Hudson Valley fois gras, tuna with wasabi, Moroccan rack of lamb, and pan-seared tiger prawns. The wine list is extensive. *Dinner (nights closed vary). Reservations essential. 239.597.3232 ext. 5666 $$$*

THE REGISTRY'S DISCO
CLUB ZANZIBAR
Naples' hottest nightclub is right at the Registry, just across from the lobby entrance and this multi-level "happening place" is packed on weekends—strobe lights, dry ice "smoke" tumbling down on the crush of dancers, everyone immersed in the latest dance craze. The second-floor balcony is packed with on lookers. If discos fit into your idea of romance, you'll love it here. If the two of you used to like these places, but think you're "too old" now, well, go on in anyway and check it out. You only live once. During the week it's a lot quieter and there's a much better chance of catching a slow song. *9 p.m.-2 a.m. Tues.-Sun., 239.597.3232 ext. 5645*

A GREAT ROMANTIC SUNDAY BRUNCH
CAFE CHABLIS
This refined and elegant Sunday brunch is one of the best-tasting and most beautifully-presented brunches ever. You'll need to dress up a bit; it's a local social event. The menu looks impressive but it doesn't even begin to cover the choices—made-to-order omelettes, waffles, several roasts, platters and platters of perfectly arranged fresh and grilled vegetables, pates, cheeses, iced shrimp, smoked oysters, chafing dishes of eggs Benedict, chicken and veal dishes, cakes and pies and cookies. Do start with a small sampling (you'll keep discovering new items you want to try) and don't check out on a Sunday if you like brunches. You'll want a lazy afternoon and a long nap after this one. *Sun. 11:30 a.m.-2:30 p.m. 239.597.3232 ext. 5828*

ROMANTIC THINGS TO DO HERE

Spend the morning or the afternoon being taken care of at the spa (239.597.3232 ext. 5607). Relax in the sauna or steam bath and then have a therapeutic massage. Or try a sea mud treatment or a seaweed full body mask.

On a calm day, rent a small boat and spend the morning offshore. Parkshore Marina *(4310 Gulf Shore Blvd. N., 239.434.0724)* rents 20' powerboats and 25' pontoon boats. A half-day for two people costs about $125.

Stop by the romantic Bistro Waterside *(Waterside Shops, 239.598.1300)* for an intimate lunch or dinner.

Browse through the upscale offerings at the nearby Waterside Shops at Pelican Bay where you'll find Saks Fifth Avenue, Ann Taylor, Banana Republic, Williams-Sonoma, and much more among waterfalls and wooden walkways. Stop in for pizza at California Pizza Kitchen.

Paddle a canoe together through the Registry's backyard. You may see blue herons, brown pelicans, roseate spoonbills, cormorants, osprey, loggerhead turtles, horseshoe crabs, and river otters.

Catch a glimpse of the Florida landscape as it used to be at the Corkscrew Swamp Sanctuary. Drive 35 minutes (get directions from the concierge) to this remarkable 11,000 acre enclave of ancient bald cypress, sawgrass marshland, pine flatwood, and cypress all managed by the National Audubon Society. A walk along the boardwalk is a showcase for tropical ferns and orchids and wading birds.

ROMANTIC RADIO
Easy: 105.1FM   Jazz: 98.9FM   Country: 107FM

HELPFUL HINTS: At the Registry, restaurant hours and days open vary with the seasons and the Brass Rail is usually only open during the winter. If you care what is open during your stay, be sure to ask in advance.

Directions: I-75, exit 107. Go west on Pine Ridge Rd. (Rt. 896), across Rt. 41 (Pine Ridge Rd. becomes Seagate Dr.) to entrance.

HELPFUL INFORMATION

LODGING RATES
The price ranges given in this book are for two people and do not include taxes or gratuities. The lower number is generally the lowest off-season rate for the smallest rooms. The higher number is generally the highest on-season rate for the nicest rooms.

Bear in mind that these are the standard rates of the properties. Off-season, and even on-season, it is well worth inquiring if there is a lower rate available or a special, off-season package. Sometimes a package will include a meal or two plus a room and the total will be less than the rate for just the room alone. In fact, all year round it is worth asking, when you are making your reservations, if there are special packages or rates available.

RESTAURANT RATES
Rates are for two people, without beverages. When a range is given, the high end is based on having all courses and choosing the highest-priced items.
$=up to $30
$$=$30-$60
$$$=over $60

HOTEL AMENITIES
In most cases, lodging descriptions in this book do not list various room amenities (coffee makers, in-room safes, bathrobes, tape players, etc.) because hotels often change their amenities. If any of these items are important to you, please ask when you are making your reservation.

DIRECTIONS
Generally, the directions at the end of each chapter are from the closest major highway directly to the lodging.

FLORIDA'S WEATHER
Summer runs from May through September, and it's pretty much the same all over the state: 90s in the day, 80s at night. Breezes along the shore keep the state's borders pleasantly cool. However, winter is generally different in various areas of Florida. Jacksonville can be about ten degrees colder than Palm Beach. The average high/low in Jacksonville in February is 66/46; in Palm Beach it's 76/65. That difference generally means that you can drive one direction and go frolicking on the beach, and drive another direction and snuggle by a fireplace. However, on any given day all winter long, all over the state, it can be sunny and in the 70s.

HELPFUL INFORMATION

AREA INFORMATION

AIRLINES & AUTOS
American 800.433.7300
Continental 800.523.3273
Delta 800.221.2121
Northwest 800.225.2525
U.S. Air 800.428.4322
Alamo 800.327.9633
Avis 800.331.1212
Hertz 800.654.3131
National 800.227.7368
Thrifty 800.367.2277

Visit Florida
661 East Jefferson St.
Tallahassee, FL 32301
Tel: 888.7FLAUSA www.flausa.com

Amelia Island COC
102 Centre St.
Fernandina Beach, FL 32035
800.226.3542 www.ameliaisland.org

Anna Maria Island/Bradenton COC
P.O. Box 100
Bradenton, FL 34206
800.462.6283
www.floridaislandbeaches.org

Cocoa Beach Area COC
400 Fortenberry Rd.
Merritt Island, FL 32952
312.459.2200 www.cocoabeachchamber.com

Daytona Beach CVB
126 E. Orange Ave.
Daytona Beach, FL 32114
800.854.1234 www.daytonabeach.com

Delray Beach COC
64 S.E. 5th Ave.
Delray Beach, FL 33483
561-278-0424 www.delraybeach.com

Fort Lauderdale CVB
1850 Eller Dr.
Fort Lauderdale, FL 33316
800.22.SUNNY www.sunny.org

Jacksonville CVB
201 E. Adams St.
Jacksonville, FL 32202
800-733-2668 www.jax.cvb

Lake Wales COC
340 W. Central Ave.
Lake Wales, FL 33859
941.676.3445
www.lakewaleschamber.com

Mount Dora COC
341 Alexander St.
Mount Dora, FL 32757
352.383.2165 www.mountdora.com

Naples Visitors Center
1074 5th Ave. S.
Naples, FL 33940
239.643.1919 www.naples-florida.com

New Smyrna Beach COC
115 Canal St.
New Smyrna Beach, FL 32168
800.541.9621
http//volusia.com/nbs

Orlando Visitor Center
8723 International Dr.
Orlando, FL 32819
800.551.0181 www.Go2orlando.com

Palm Beach CVB
155 Palm Beach Lakes Blvd.
W. Palm Beach, FL 33401
800.554.7256 www.palmbeachfl.com

Palm Island/Charlotte County CVB
1600 Tamiami Trail
Port Charlotte, FL 33948
800.478.7352 www.Pureflorida.com

Sanibel Visitors Center
1159 Causeway Rd.
Sanibel, FL 33957
941.472.1080
www.sanibelflorida.com

Sarasota Visitor Information Center
6551 N. Tamiami Trail
Sarasota, FL 34236
800.522.9799 www.sarasotafl.org

Seaside COC
County Rd. 30-A (Box 4730)
Santa Rosa Beach, FL 32459
888.SEASIDE www.seasidefl.com

St. Augustine/St. John's County CVB
88 Riberia St.
St. Augustine, FL 32084
800.OLD.CITY www.visitoldcity.com

Tallahassee Visitors Bureau
106 E. Jefferson St.
Tallahassee, FL 32302
800.628.2866 www.seeTallahassee.com

Winter Park COC
150 N. New York Ave.
Winter Park, FL 32789
407.644.8281 www.ci.winter-park.fl.us

INDEX

ABOUT THE AUTHORS

Since escaping corporate jobs in Manhattan over a decade ago, husband and wife team Pam Acheson and Dick Myers have explored, lived in, and written about romantic Florida and the Caribbean.

Between them, they have authored, written, and contributed to over sixty books and written articles for dozens of national and international magazines. They founded and published a daily newspaper in the British Virgin Islands for six years. They have been featured guests on television and radio shows throughout the United States and the Caribbean.

Their knowledgeable, personal, reader-friendly guides to romantic Florida, the British Virgin Islands, and the U.S. Virgin Islands perennially rank among the best sellers for these destinations in the world.

Dick and Pam are currently working on their newest book, *The Best Romantic Escapes In the Caribbean*.

When they are not on the road, they divide their time between the British Virgin Islands and the Sunshine State. They also quite enjoy visiting Manhattan.

More great reviews for
The Best Romantic Escapes in Florida
series

"Pamela Acheson and Dick Myers are the quintessential experts on romantic Florida."
—*Hugh Benjamin*
author, A Place Like This

"A lighthearted guidebook...full of insider tips and recommendations."   —*Essentially America*

"Lush locales and exquisite eateries...also tips on how to best prepare for a romantic trip to paradise."   —*Ft. Lauderdale Sun-Sentinel*

"Pick up *The Best Romantic Escapes in Florida.* Acheson and Myers tell you where to stay, eat, drink, dance, and more."   —*St. Petersburg Times*

"Unique, informative, with humor sprinkled throughout."   —*Buffalo News*

"Romantic choices for everyone, from small inns and quaint hotels to barefoot beach escapes and sophisticated seaside resorts."—*Midwest Book Review*

"This is a great book."   —*NBC News 2 Midday*